WORTH

PURPOSE BEYOND AMBITION

CONTENTS

ACKNOWLEDGMENTS

For my precious wife, my loving daughter, son on the way, and those whom I may innocently glance at a bit too long – to witness their gifts.

Above all, I thank God. I had never realized until recently his presence by my side, especially during this journey, keeping me safe and constantly revealing, where there is darkness there is light.

Introduction: Thief of Temporary Happiness

"Start by doing what's necessary; then do what's possible;

and suddenly you are doing the impossible."

—*St. Francis of Assisi*

***

Writing, unfortunately, doesn't come naturally to me. In fact, sometimes, it's an overwhelming and long process; it can take me hours to write a few pages. At the same time, it's been nearly a decade since I felt compelled to write this book. **As if God were continually tapping me on the shoulder for the last ten years,** I feel I was given a series of "nudges" that eventually pushed me to put the experiences and revelations of my journey into writing. One of these pivotal moments was an interesting experience in Mexico City in 2010 while giving a lecture at one of the top Universities in Mexico, called Tec de Monterrey.

Tec de Monterrey is Mexico's top-ranked business and medical school with partnerships all around the world, and I had been invited there on several occasions as a guest lecturer. My first talk, even though in English, apparently went well, and the professor of Business and Economics graciously invited me back to speak on the topics of entrepreneurship, my humanitarian work across South America, and social leadership. However, on this day, the lecture I was delivering was called "The Thief of Temporary Happiness."

Although I had built a few businesses by then, I didn't want to allude that success in business or even in a career was the golden ticket to a fulfilling and meaningful life. They needed to be highly conscious of several things, and how they fulfill happiness and purpose in their lives was definitely one of them.

In my humble opinion, the meaning of "success" is distorted, and if we aren't careful, we can easily become wrapped up in short-lived accomplishments, labels, and material trappings, never realizing our true potential and purpose until it's too late. **Only then will we realize that we've sacrificed a disproportionate amount of our lives to the thief of temporary happiness.**

As I walked out onto the stage that day, I looked out at the familiar faces of the beautiful students. They were quieter and more attentive than usual. I assumed this was because of the enigmatic title of the talk that day. They had also come to know that I never approached two lectures in the same way. But the one constant was my focus on being 100% present with them so that I could expand their perspectives and fuel their hearts and minds.

As I took the stage, I took a moment to calibrate as I found my spot next to the podium. I was standing in a beautiful lecture hall behind a carved wood podium about four feet off the ground on a crescent shaped stage. The university crest in bronze hung on the wall. It was a beautiful room. Mexico was so different than expected; sometimes, I wondered how I ended up here.

A year prior, in 2009, after my wife and I married, I had told her we could live anywhere we wanted. Our top choices were Argentina, Japan, or France. But during that time, a friend of mine who had been living in Mexico City graciously invited me to come visit him so he could show me how he saw Mexico. He showed me more than the city itself; he showed me the heart of Mexico City: the people, the culture, the friendships, (let's not forget about the food!), and the desire they had to get stronger and better together. With all of this, I was absolutely blown away. It was a moment when my understanding had been opened up to see through the lens of someone else's perspectives. I realized that I hadn't noticed so many things at first glance. Like him, I never wanted to leave.

Long story short, we chose Mexico City. ¡Viva México!

Within weeks, my wife and I found a beautiful home in the neighborhood of Polanco and moved in. It was a very nice area with several important embassies scattered throughout and literally within walking distance to everything: major commercial areas, gyms, markets, etc. In some ways, it was the Beverly Hills of Mexico City, mixed with some of the most beautiful parks and greenery I'd ever seen. What struck me immediately was how sociable the people were here. They weren't always quiet or reserved, and something was always happening in the city to experience. The city was a bit crazy at times (but I like crazy), and I was amazed at how close friends were here. I loved the warmth of the culture. And, as I alluded to before, the food was fantastic. At that time, I was still running my second company remotely, but I had an itch to start doing much more. And one of the channels to do that was through teaching and executive coaching.

So, there I was at Tec de Monterrey with my few notes, looking out over the sea of eager faces. I was a bit overwhelmed that day because the topic felt almost as if it had a greater purpose. Within a few minutes into the lecture, I noticed I had one hundred percent of their attention. With this, I decided to take pause, bow my head with a prayer, and sit quietly on the edge of the stage. *This is the time to go deeper,* I thought, *and give of myself, as if they were my own family, with a lesson and story that could possibly help transform and enrich their life for the greater good.* Even if some didn't understand it, **I wanted to make sure that they understood that I *cared* about each of them more than how perfectly my talk went.**

I began my talk that day sharing with the students some experiences I had during my missionary work in South America in 2006. I told them a story about traveling in Peru where I'd see children as young as two, selling candies and other wares in the streets with their mothers. What I found fascinating is that these kids typically didn't look sad or deprived of love; from what I could see, they seemed generally happy.

As I worked on the day centers and orphanages in this country, sometimes, I would see these same kids in school during the day. They would come in dirty, with ripped and worn clothing. Others had rotting teeth, smelled of urine, with hair matted and filled with soil. They were obviously lacking some basic necessities, but their situation was not to define them. Later in the afternoon, I would see them with their mothers working. Sometimes, I wouldn't see them at school at all.

I know it isn't right to take a child out of school to work in the streets, but I considered another perspective, *this child is with his or her mother all day, getting attention and love in brief moments throughout the day.* Most of the children in my home country of Canada were well-educated but struggled to gain the love and patience needed from their parents who had careers, responsibilities, and demands of their own as well as priorities and goals for their own sense of purpose and meaning. Compared to what I saw in Peru and most of South America, where the children always had their parents close by, Western families (not all, but some) would at times become disconnected and temporarily lost in other pursuits.

This was a constant theme in my travels as I went to Peru, Argentina, Chile, Uruguay, Venezuela, and Colombia. I would see some families with three kids, a mother, and a father all living in one room. Compared to Western standards, it was the size of a walk-in closet. But if you were there as well, you would also witness their peaceful smiles as they conversed lovingly and without mental distraction. They were always together in the early morning and right after work, at an hour when people in my country were usually trying to catch up with what they expect life should be.

The families I saw didn't have much to boast about material wise, but they had these moments of togetherness, when they were connected by just being present with one another. I found their smiles and laughter honest and contagious. Even the way they walked and carried themselves was engaging because it wasn't forced or contrived. In contrast, if you go into any metropolitan space in North America, people tend to be a bit tense and far more distant, but more disheartening, they unknowingly avoid making eye contact, even with their loved ones.

I asked to the students, "Who has the better foundation of life?"

My question must have sparked their curiosity because after the talk, as several of them lined up to share a few moments more. At the end of the line stood two young men who would soon ask me a question, one that stays with me even to this day.

I would soon learn these young men were from the ultra-high net worth circles in Mexico and were both 17-years-old. It's important to note that the wealthy families I was exposed to in Mexico often looked more European, and these boys were no exception. They were dressed immaculately. One had bright blonde hair, and a pink sweater draped over his shoulders. The other was tall, with very fair skin and blue eyes. As they drew closer, both stood with their arms crossed properly across their chests, matching gold Rolex watches on their wrists.

They waited patiently for me to finish with the others, but I could tell they were slightly anxious and conflicted with their question. I could see it in their eyes when I glanced over. With that, I had a moment of doubt—*do I have the answer?*

One of them apprehensively said, "We heard your talk, and it made a lot of sense, but there's something we can't figure out..."

"What is it?"

The young men looked at each other.

"Can people with no money be happy?"

It was a simple question, but it really took me aback. Because for me, the answer was clearly yes. But I'd never really phrased it this way. Once, I would have said no to that question. And now, I was wondering how much the idea that money was a primary driver to happiness had been driving these young men and others.

They had no worries (at least, from the outside looking in). I later learned that one was the son of a Forbes list billionaire. They had round-the-clock drivers waiting for them outside the university, ready to take them wherever they wanted to go with their parents' seemingly limitless credit card and return them safely to their guarded estates, regardless the hour. To me, they were in a completely different universe. From where they were standing, they believed that to be happy and a person of importance, you had to be successful, and to be successful you had to: a) come from a wealthy family; b) have the best education, or; c) bend the rules from time to time to get what you want.

My experience was completely different, and I found their question fascinating. As they did mine.

The reality is, I didn't grow up with an abundance of money or even access to the resources. After my parents divorced when I was 7 years old, I lived with my mother, who was struggling to raise my younger brother and me alone. We were so poor that, sometimes, we lived out of hotels or slept in a tent in the park. As an adult, I never wanted to be in a situation without money. I believed I had to be self-reliant and figure out a way to always take care of myself and those closest to me, since growing up relying on those around me wasn't always the best (or safest) option.

As a result, I believed striving for success was the only way to be someone of importance, to give my own children what they would need, and to be at peace.

After high school, I moved to Toronto with my girlfriend. We lived in a single room while I was working at Taco Bell and taking classes at night for graphic design. Eventually, I took a job as a silk screen printer, while continuing my studies. After gaining different experiences at various companies, I left my job as a Senior Graphic Designer at a prominent agency and started my own marketing agency. The same year I started my company, I married my high school sweetheart, and I finally felt I was on the track to becoming a successful entrepreneur. But just like a lot of other people, as I grew more successful in my business, I slowly fell into the trap of believing that an increase in material wealth would bring me closer to being happy, fulfilled, and safe.

The straw that broke the camel's back, so to speak, was when we bought our dream house.

I remember very clearly looking for a new home; the real estate agent drove us up the long driveway and parked in the round-about in front of a beautiful house in an upscale area of Caledon, just outside of Toronto. With a few exotic cars parked in the driveway, my wife and I got out of our Volkswagen Jetta, and stood facing the front entrance in awe. I saw the place and thought, *There's no way...*

We walked into the chalet-type mansion with cathedral ceilings that went three levels up in the entryway. The entire back wall was all glass, with a wraparound balcony overlooking three acres of landscaped backyard that included an apple orchard with thirty-five apple trees.

It was totally out of our price range.

The real estate agent said, "Oh, I know it's outside your budget, but you never know."

After the tour I stood in the kitchen, looking out over the gardens. It was breathtaking. I was thinking, *I guess I could increase my salary. We could make it work, but it would be difficult; I would have to put in extra hours at the office.*

I don't know how she knew, but the agent pointed out the window and said, "See that neighborhood over there?"

I knew the area she was referring to: the poor part of town.

"Wouldn't it be cool if those kids over there said, 'Hey Mom, I want to go play with the rich kids!'"

I had been one of "those kids" over there. I remember wanting to play in nice houses with the rich kids, who seemingly had everything. After she said that, I felt a weight pulling down on my heart. It was something that drove me to success most of my life: I didn't want my kids growing up feeling they were never enough, let alone excluded.

I swore I would figure it out.

We paid $740,000 for the house, and this was over fifteen years ago when the average home was $315,000 in Toronto. It was a monumental jump for us. I still remember looking out the back window in the morning and watching the deer stroll through the apple orchards on our property. It was our dream house. Sometimes, when I go back to Caledon, I drive by. Tragically, we only lived there for six months.

What I didn't know back then was that when you base your life and worth on accumulating material things, you build walls around yourself. It isolates you. My marriage was on the verge of crumbling. My wife and I began to distract ourselves by connecting with material things that made us feel important, instead of connecting with each other, and the house was the tipping point. Meanwhile, my business was taking off, and I continued to fill my life with things to fill that growing void. I would go out on shopping sprees and drop $500 or $1,000 on a dress shirt, because I could. Growing up poor, this was a big deal to me. I bought a motorcycle, and then another. Then I bought my dream car, a dark blue convertible Porsche that I parked next to my wife's Jag. Even though I was in the office quite a bit, I had a long-standing open account at a day spa, where I would spend a full day when I needed to destress and feel "important."

One day, I went to pick up my dad in my new car to take him for a spin. I remember driving with each of my fingers curled down, one after another, around the steering wheel as I accelerated with anticipation, bracing for the next curve in the road, exhilarated that I was able to experience the "happiness" and the thrill of driving. Being 30 years old and driving my first Porsche always gave me a sense of accomplishment and pride. It was also a reminder of how far I'd come from living in parks and shelters as a child.

Suddenly, my father looked at me and said, **"Erik, my son, most of the things you're chasing bring you only temporary happiness, and these exciting things are slowly trapping you."**

He said it softly, in a passive conversational tone, but I never really understood what he meant till later in life.

I remember thinking at the time, *Whatever, Dad. You were never as successful as I am. You're a chef; you never had your own company. You work for someone else and don't own half of the things I do.*

I'm glad I didn't say it out loud, thinking back now; I was embarrassingly arrogant in my youth.

The thing is, he was right. It's like I was suffering from a suffocating addiction. First, I chased the money, then got the house, then I got the car, now I needed the designer suit, the shoes, the watch, etc. It never ended for me back then. And if people asked me what I did, I'd proudly say—I own my own company. This is where I live, and this is what I owned, thinking it defined my value as a person. I had based my entire identity, my self-worth, my position among others on my accomplishments for my own glory.

When the thrill of owning the latest new thing inevitably wore off, I started to feel disillusioned. Sure, I had most of the things I dreamt of owning, but, over time, I also became increasingly bored. It was never enough. And my father, a humble executive chef, who was as proud of his sparkling clean kitchen floors and the pride his dishwasher took in his job as I was of my Porsche, could see right through it. **I had trusted the "thief of temporary happiness."**

Not long after this, I got the idea to go to Peru. I remember the moment very clearly.

One day, I was sitting in my office in Toronto, laptop open, blankly staring at the screen. Half of my office was packed up already, my desk was surrounded by boxes. In the course of a month, my wife and I had separated, I'd sold the company, put my house on the market, and gotten rid of most of my belongings (except the Porsche). The new owner gave me a good exit package that included a salary for the next six months as part of a humble earn out. My life was in transition, but I was no longer seemingly trapped.

As soon as I began stepping away from all the luxurious clutter I had been drowning in, a little voice inside me said, "You gotta' go." Increasingly each day, I felt the urge to leave the environment I had come to know and do so much more, but, this time, not for financial gain. I wanted to volunteer and find those children who had started out in similar situations as I did, who were in extreme poverty, who were abandoned, or who had faced extreme violence and worse. I was getting a decent amount of money in the package, but it wasn't as if I could go out and buy a yacht and travel the world, *so where did I want to go?* I thought about going to South America, somewhere

I'd always wanted to see, like Peru. And I wanted to help abandoned and impoverished children.

I remember excitedly searching the Web until I found a place I could volunteer at in Peru. Even though I'd volunteered with children for many years in Canada with Big Brothers, L-Arche, and YMCA, this was something very new to me. It was an orphanage and a day center for kids in a town called Ayacucho, and I planned to go for a week. You had to pay to volunteer, which was strange to me. But I was excited because I'd finally found something to start the journey. **Frankly, I was also scared. I was 31, but I'd never traveled outside of Canada alone.** Also, I didn't speak a lick of Spanish. Not even the words "cerveza" or "gracias" were in my vocabulary.

But I thought, *if it scares me and it's good for me, and good for others too, then I must!* With that idea pushing me, I said to myself (I was literally talking to myself), "What would happen if I go for *three* weeks?"

My heart started pounding. I'd heard all these rumors about South American countries with people getting kidnapped or worse. My mind filled with potential scenarios, and none of them looked safe or smart.

"No, no. That's crazy," I said.

I scrolled down and then noticed they had a month-long program. I asked myself, "Well...what happens if I go for a *month*?"

Now my palms really started to sweat. *What if I get stuck there and can't come back? What if someone tries to drug me, rob me, or worse?* This was really freaking me out. But it was like watching a horror movie—it was frightening and curiously exciting all at once.

Then I got a really crazy idea. I asked myself, "What happens if I go to more than one country?" Then I could serve more children, not just the ones who are abandoned or poor; I could work with all different types of disadvantaged children. I felt a question bubbling up from deep inside of me, finally it broke the surface. ***What is the one thing that all children need to create a better quality of life? I had to find out.***

With this driving purpose, one that moved my blood, the fear slipped away, effortlessly.

I instantly booked the trip to Peru and spent the next three months traveling through South America, working at shelters and orphanages and interviewing the owners and leadership to learn more about their issues, opportunities, and challenges. In all, I went to Peru, Chile, Argentina, Uruguay, Venezuela, and Colombia. Everywhere, I found the piece that had been missing from my life. Happiness isn't dependent on money; it's *more* than money. It's more than the "things" we "get" and accomplish. Saying we're happy and feeling like we're somebody important because we can point to our accomplishments doesn't make us any more connected to others. It actually separates us.

What we see on the surface is only 1% of a person's gift and what they have to give. There is always far more richness and depth that we don't see underneath. And what really matters is intangible; our connection to people around us and the quality of that connection is directly tied to the beliefs about ourselves and others. If we really want to feel love and our value, we have to strive to see it in others first. And that requires looking deeper into the miracles we're all given with greater courage, patience, and curiosity and far less fear, control, and judgment.

Saying we're happy and feeling like we're somebody important because we can point to our accomplishments doesn't make us any more connected to others. It separates us.

***

After the tour across South, I had uncovered the answer to that question of what all children need to have a better quality of life, more so, what all of us need to have a better quality of life. In addition, I had the treasured opportunity to share precious and timeless moments with hundreds of children, inspiring leaders, and friends along this journey. When I returned, I eventually started another company, remarried, and my life and purpose continued to unfold. Still, these experiences have imprinted a new code in my heart and mind to the point of a purpose-driven obsession. Years later, I still found myself circling toward that simple question those two boys asked me that day in Mexico City: Can people be happy without money?

How many people were out there striving to live a life of temporary happiness, just like I had been?

I wondered what would happen if I shared my experiences with others, or potentially the world. Even though I'm not a writer by profession, I started a blog. Within a few months, I had 400,000 views and 220,000 followers on Facebook. The stories were very real, and, to my surprise, people responded to them, many times with their own questions, and I made a point to respond to as many as possible. I shared everything, even the embarrassing mistakes I'd made. One day, I was reflecting on my blogs and realized I had actually written enough content for a book.

As you may already be aware, this isn't a book about material success, the fight, or the lessons or triumphs of my work as a business person. This book, these stories, written over the last ten years, are a compilation of life-transforming events and lessons that unlocked my eyes and heart as I journeyed across South America. I wrote this book for several reasons. First, I wanted to reflect on the extraordinary experiences that I took in, like a sip from a fire hose, that transformed my entire life: the way I live, love, teach, work, and see the world—everything.

Secondly, I'm writing this book for my daughter and for our second child on the way. This record of my heart's and mind's journey is for them so that when they grow up, they can learn what my father also taught me, along with the gifts and pathway God has opened for all of us.

In the following chapters, you may find inspiration. You may find greater depth and strength toward your own purpose. Or maybe you'll begin to look at and appreciate yourself and others in a more profound way and gain a few tools to go beyond the 1% that is seen or projected and ultimately uncover and experience the priceless gifts of happiness, fulfillment, and joy that surround all of us and is already within us all.

Please understand, I'm not looking to change anyone with this one book. All I ask is that you walk with me on this journey as a new potential friend, with an open hand, a curious mind, and a hungry heart as I share each of these life experiences with heartfelt love, a new sense of compassion, and unbridled humility. And if what we shared here together helped a small handful of our brothers and sisters for the greater good, then I believe that, together, we would have impacted our future and theirs more than either of us could ever possibly imagine.

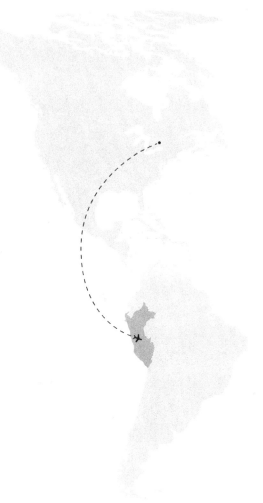

Part One
Peru:
A Punch to The
Heart

March 2006
Toronto International Airport

***

T rying to orient myself, I stepped into the Toronto International Airport departures lobby with a single, four-foot long backpack strapped to my body and walked into the middle of the chaos. In front of me were screens with rotating schedules, an array of travelers dashing across the floor rushing to their destinations, and people of all backgrounds, ages, and styles. To me, back then, the space was massive, intimidating, and incredibly confusing.

After a few moments of awkwardly standing in people's way and looking at my papers neatly organized for the first flight, I spotted the directions for my airline, and made my way to the aisle to stand in line at the ticket counter. As I reached the front of the line, the woman behind the desk on the far right looked over her black rimmed glasses at me and signaled with a quick hand gesture to approach.

"Where are you going?"

"Peru…" I replied. After a delicate pause, I added, "Lima."

She stood there looking at me expectantly, waiting for me to do something. I had no idea what she wanted.

"Your ID, sir?"

"Yes, I'm sorry..."

Awkwardly, I swung my oversized backpack around to the front and proceeded to scramble through the pockets. I felt my face get warm and my shoulders tense as she watched me in silence. Finally, I found it and handed it to the attendant.

She checked my passport and handed it back to me with my ticket to Peru. A moment or two later she looked up from the computer with a slight annoyance and surprise, as I was still standing there.

"Sir, you have to go now."

"Where?" I asked politely.

"To your gate," she said, pointing to the far end of the building.

I walked away feeling embarrassed yet excited to embark on my mission.

At the departure gate, I threw my things on the seat next to me and sat down. I had half an hour to kill before we boarded the plane. Nearby was a small newsstand with snacks and magazines, but my mind was racing far too much to eat anything. Thinking back, it makes me smile. I must have looked like Forrest Gump sitting there in the departure gate waiting area—someone could have taken my wallet, slipped something into my bag, anything—I was entrenched in my thoughts, completely focused on what was to come, and yet totally oblivious.

Although I had been outside of Canada before, this was the first time I'd ever flown alone. Normally, my wife Andrea was with me, and she handled all the travel arrangements. In our marriage, I had always been in charge of the business and home finances, and Andrea took care of everything else. At the time, there were moments I felt a bit lost without her.

Only a few short months ago I had a loving wife, a beautiful estate home on two acres of land, and my own growing agency...

Sitting there in the airport, my thoughts drifted back to the day I told Andrea I wanted to separate. It was our wedding anniversary, and shamefully, I had forgotten. In my unprepared youth, I believed I had fallen out of love, and two years prior I was totally caught up in thinking about how to fix the situation. It all came to a halt on that Saturday morning in early December. I was standing on the long staircase that went through the middle of the house, watching her slowly come up the stairs and stop less than a foot in front of me.

Time stopped. **My head sank as if a great painful weight were pulling it down, and I simply said, "I think we should separate."**

She stood there looking up at me in silence. In that moment I saw the girl I'd married and saw her heart break. I realized that not only was this a total surprise to her, but it was far more painful than when I had played it out in my head. Later, we sat at the kitchen table and cried and held each other. After a lot of listening and answering each other, she eventually agreed. That night she went to her mother's house. Both of us knew it was over.

Over the months to come, it was very hard for both of us to be apart, even when attempting to date other people. I'd grown up with my wife, we'd been together since we were kids (17 years old), that was more than half my adult life. In some ways, she was literally the only person who knew me. I'm sure she felt similarly, because even after the divorce, we were still friends. In fact, I had given her the Porsche to drive while I went on this trip.

Now, I was alone at the airport with a one-way ticket to a foreign country, alone and without a plan.

I reviewed the situation at hand. In some ways I was confident because I had a purpose, but I literally had no itinerary after Peru. I knew that on the first night, I would stay in Lima, but that was it.

All those countries I planned on visiting after Peru, I had no idea where I'd stay while I was working there. I did my best to arrange things online before leaving, as I knew Internet access once in South America would be a different story. **Back then, hotels, businesses, and Internet cafes with Wi-Fi weren't as widespread in South America as they are now.** It was all on me to figure it out.

Normally, I stayed in five-star hotels, but I didn't think it would be congruent to go back to my luxury hotel after spending all day working in the poorest of communities or with abandoned children, so I'd agreed to stay in the lodging provided by the first organization that I'd arranged to volunteer with. I was nervous about what the living conditions were, as there were no photos or descriptions of any kind.

Twenty more minutes before boarding. I sat back in my seat and tried to imagine the people I might meet in Peru, especially the children. I was a bit worried about how I would communicate with them, not knowing any Spanish. I wondered if the kids would think, *Who is this guy showing up here?*

A month before I decided to go to Peru, I met a Colombian woman on PerfectMatch.com who lived nearby in Hamilton, Ontario and we'd become very close in heart and mind in a short time. Before I left, she translated a letter I had written into Spanish, so I could read it personally, to the children at every orphanage and nonprofit organization I went to.

The letter was a simple introduction about me written for them. *Who am I?* I wanted to tell them that even though I'm from Canada, thousands of miles away, I've gone through similar things as they have, and that they weren't alone and there's hope and purpose for them. Most importantly, I wanted to tell them: no matter how dire your situation may be, you aren't disadvantaged, you aren't alone, and you are somebody with a unique gift and purpose.

Lima, Peru
Smiling Faces and Dark Places

***

I got off the plane in Lima and entered the airport. I was so excited and anxious, I remember I wore all black.

Back then, I typically dressed only in designer suits, Armani, Hugo Boss, and Versace, but I had tried to tone it down for my trip to South America to look more appropriate and humbler. I was dressed in black jeans and a black t-shirt with a simple black jacket over it.

The first night in Peru, I had a desire to go to a club (I never went to clubs). Even though I dressed as a punk and listened to alternative music in high school, and most people assumed I drank and smoked because of the way I looked, in reality, I had always been pretty straight edge and fairly responsible. At the time, even during this journey, I was on a strict diet that excluded caffeine, meat, dairy, and sugar, and I almost never drank. But I thought it would be nice to see what the music was like in a different culture, and I wanted to be around people. So, I immediately thought of a nightclub.

I went down to the lobby of the hotel and asked for a taxi, which wasn't too difficult. I was happy to discover "taxi" was a universal word in Spanish and English. I jumped in the back of the cab and the driver said something to me in Spanish. **From the blank look on my face, he quickly realized I had no plans, and no idea where I wanted to go** (we didn't have phone apps back then).

I decided to improvise. I put my hands up as if I were dancing, and said, "Club?"

The driver gave me a puzzled look. I tried to think of another word, so I said, "Music? Disco?"

Finally, a light of recognition came into his eyes. He nodded his head, "Yes, yes...¿disco? ¿chicas?"

"Yes."

"¡Ah...okey, Señor!"

Sitting back in my seat I thought, *Great! He understands me.*

Lima is the capital of Peru, and I was able to take in an eyeful of the city as we drove. At first, we passed through the downtown area with its lively plazas and colorful colonial Spanish style buildings, then, after some time, we started to enter a more industrial and less touristy looking area on the outskirts. **I tried not to worry, but the further we got from the lights of the city, the more my concern grew.**

Finally, the driver pulled up to a large building and stopped the car. We were in front of a warehouse, maybe three stories high, all one color outside, with very few windows. I noticed there weren't many cars in the parking lot. In front of the entrance were several intimidating-looking bouncers staring at us. I thought, *This is one of those exclusive places!*

I paid the driver and exited the taxi. The bouncer took my money, opened the steel doors, and ushered me inside and up a stairway to the second floor. The instant I walked inside, I saw a bare stage in the center of the room, and about fifteen women sitting on couches around it, barely clothed. The second they saw me, they all stood up.

I'm not in the right place.

Immediately, I thanked the waiter who greeted me, turned around, and went back downstairs. However, the cab driver was gone. *Great.* I was in the middle of nowhere, and now I was really worried. The bouncers were asking me where I was going, and nobody could understand a word that was coming out of my mouth. It took me a while to get out of there.

Thankfully, I'm a sharp student, and after this I learned my lesson. With the word "chicas," I had to be careful of the context.

The second night in Lima, I decided to try and go to a club again. I had packed lightly, just a backpack for three months, so I had the same outfit on. Same as the night before, I got into the cab and said, "Disco?"

But this time, I added, "No mas chicas."

The driver looked puzzled. "¿Chicas?"

"No, *mas* chicas," I repeated. (Apparently, I was misusing the word "mas" that I found in my English to Spanish Dictionary. I thought it meant "a lot.")

He looked at me confused at first, and then in the rearview mirror, I could see him look up at me. He tilted his head, squinted his eyes (as if he'd come to some important conclusion about me), and said, "¡Ahhhh…okey, Señor!"

This time, we drove into the heart of Lima, right downtown, to what appeared to be a newer club in a livelier area. We pulled up to a big black building, probably a half a block wide, a huge warehouse. You could hear the thump of the bass beat from the outside, it sounded like techno or some sort of dance music. I thought, *Great, finally.*

I walked in the front door and went down a long dark hallway. About half way, down a few guys appeared, walking beside me. I said, "Hola."

In Peru, I'm generally tall, so I wasn't feeling intimidated by them. But I thought it was a little strange. Also strange was the way they were dressed—they were wearing undershirts and chains—it was definitely a different dress code. Once inside, I walked up to the bar and ordered the safest thing to drink. There were a lot of guys there, but I figured I must be early. I stood there sipping on my drink, smiling, and looking around. Some of the guys were looking back at me.

Then I realized that they were *really* looking at me. *Wait a minute...*

No, no, no.

I ended up leaving respectfully and quietly, leaving my unfinished beverage on the bar. Once outside, I crossed the street and went over to an outdoor bar and sat down at one of the tables on the patio, feeling as if I had just learned another lesson. There was an older man at a table next to me and we struck up a conversation. He was from the U.S., a commercial S.C.U.B.A. diver. He told me about exploring sunken ships and I told him about my misadventures with the clubs— one was all women, and the other was all men. We both laughed. It was quite an experience.

After a nice chat and a beer, I went back to my hotel. The next morning, I would head to the airport and fly to Ayacucho, my first destination, and onto the mission.

As I lay in bed that night, it dawned on me that while I had seen a lot of things in business and in life, I still had plenty to learn about the world around me. Looking back, I was very naive.

Ayacucho, Peru
The Boy in the Box
✳✳✳

"There are always flowers for those who want to see them."
—Henri Matisse

Compared to Lima, arriving in the small town of Ayacucho was like traveling back in time.

Ayacucho was nestled in the central highlands of Peru, a fertile valley that was home to little more than 180,000 people. Many of the famous cathedrals and buildings were built in the 17th century. As I walked down the cracked and well-worn roads, I could get a sense of the people and the Peruvian culture underneath the tides of Spanish colonization and political strife.

I immediately understood what they meant by "basic" when I walked into the hostel. It was a narrow structure, just three rooms with concrete walls and floors, one for eating, one for sleeping, and a small closet-like room that had a hose and bucket—the "shower" room. **The "beds" in the sleeping room were two feet wider than your hips, made of a metal frame.** Since we had to make this one room work – the beds were squeezed side by side, only inches apart. A piece of cardboard lay on top to sleep on, but you had to use a sleeping bag, so the metal bars wouldn't poke into your back as you slept.

That first night, trying to sleep in a room with twenty or so odd strangers—all with different levels of hygiene and nasal issues—was definitely an experience. A couple of times, I woke up with someone's foot in my side, or an arm in my face.

In the morning, as I splashed cold water from a bucket on my body and hosed myself down. (there was no electricity for hot water), I realized I didn't mind it so much. I was grateful to finally start my journey and take action on what I always felt compelled to do: help and serve children who were the underdogs so to speak, like I had been in my childhood. Finally, my dream to give back was coming true.

I must admit, I was still a little concerned that I didn't speak Spanish. But I took comfort knowing that our fears can keep us trapped and, if left unchallenged, limit us from experiencing the gift of life and all that *we* have to offer. I was ready to see what lay beyond the comfortable, safe corner of the world I'd always known.

The first day I went to the day center, it was immediately clear it wasn't the most modern of facilities. The building was a bit run down, the paint was peeling, and the walls were bare. You could easily see it was a subsidized place, but for me it was absolutely beautiful. **This was the first gateway into the whole experience of service work, and I fell in love with it instantly.**

Even though it was a busy morning, the people running the facility took time to show me around the daycare. They spoke to me in Spanish, unbothered by the fact that I couldn't understand what they said. We did have one person translating for us (in very broken English), and from what I gathered, the parents of the children could drop off their kids while they were out working during the day. I also knew some of the kids were coming from impoverished situations, but I wasn't quite prepared for what I saw.

There majority of the kids were around three to five years old, but there were some newborns, and some older kids up to ten years old. The children arrived, some of them without shoes, one girl smelled strongly of urine, and some of the boys had rotten teeth from sucking on local sugar cane. When they smiled, I could see brown gaps between their front teeth. But the second I saw them, I lit up. **For me, what state they were in wasn't as important**

as who they were. I enjoyed them all (even the ones who hadn't had a bath in weeks).

That first day, we did simple volunteer activities with the kids. It was very procedural with a lot of "this is what we're doing now" and "this is what we'll do later." We sat at the small tables with the children while they did a range of activities such as puzzles, drawing, or singing. We'd be helping them with some math and basic writing that day, and, later, the volunteers would be free to go out for dinner as a group. In the evenings, we were on our own.

At mealtime, I had a chance to interact with some of the other volunteers and discovered they were from many different parts of the world. It felt like everyone there was trying to get something different out of their experience. Some, like me, were at a transition point in their life, and others had motives that weren't so clear. I met a guy from New York who was a frustrated cook who quit his job. Another woman had kids of her own, and all else I knew of her was that she was from France. One gentleman from the UK was highly academic but was taking a break from university. One was an artist trying to find meaning in her life.

The volunteer program was only four weeks long, and I wouldn't have enough time to get to know each of their stories as in depth as I'd like to. I knew some would take more from the program than others. As for me, I was determined to focus as much on the children as I could. Every morning, I'd wake up just before dawn, wash up as best I could, and head straight over to the day center, so I could spend as much time as possible working with the children. **After a few days of this, I started to notice several new things.**

One day, I saw a little boy, sitting against the wall. He wasn't playing with the others. Although his outward appearance looked normal—he was clean and clothed—he was quite isolated, like he didn't want to engage with anyone. I walked over and squatted down next to him.

I said, "Hola." He was silent.

I wasn't sure what to do, so I changed my approach several times. I offered him my hand so we could walk over to where the other kids were. He wouldn't take it, he just sat there. I had my camera with me, and I tried to show him a picture the other children had taken. He glanced for a moment at the screen and then turned his face away. He wouldn't engage.

With patience, I tried to play with him in several respectful ways, but I couldn't get a smile or any response, good or bad at all. With all the others I had spent time with, I could at least get them to smile and just be a kid for a moment, but he was like a statue. No more than five years old, and his heart had gone numb. He was like a boy made of stone.

I was both curious and heartbroken, as if I was punched in the heart to truly understand. I had a sense of what he was feeling, but I couldn't put words to it. I decided to take a picture of him from afar, because for some reason I wanted to remember him. *I can't forget this boy,* I thought. I really wanted to tell him he was somebody important in this life.

There was something else, a look in his eyes that I'd seen before, as if he'd been through something traumatic, and now someone (or something) else was taking over. He was disconnected.

It reminded me of an image I had of myself as a child. I've never been the type to dwell on my childhood—I've always seen myself as being responsible for myself, not a victim—but years ago, in my twenties, I thought it might be interesting to see a therapist, although I don't remember the specific reason why. This particular therapist did what was called timeline therapy. During our sessions, she asked me, "If you picture yourself as a young boy, what does it look like?"

I closed my eyes and saw myself as a young boy in a big room, inside a box. The image was vivid, but also painful. The lid of the box was closed, and it was dark inside, but I never wanted to come out of it. Sometimes I'd lift the lid a little, and look out and see nobody, but still I was scared to come out.

Every time I tried to picture my childhood, I saw this little boy in a box. I even sketched it out on a piece of paper, a little boy curled up inside a box. The therapist made me go back to my earliest thoughts until I was able to move forward through my timeline. I didn't have a major catharsis in these sessions, so I'm not sure I got much out of it other than this visual metaphor for my childhood, which was accurate in that I was often lonely and uncertain. I hadn't thought about the "boy in the box" until this boy in Ayacucho triggered my memory of that feeling.

I knew instantly what he was doing; he was completely withdrawing to save himself from feeling anything. To allow himself to open up at the risk of being hurt would be catastrophic.

I wished I could tell this little boy that whatever darkness he was in, however he might be trapped, *it's not forever; you can get out of this.* Even though I couldn't speak Spanish, I wanted to find a way to communicate this to him. I couldn't stop myself, I felt drawn to try and support him again and again. Whenever I tried to interact with him, I felt my heart hurt, but I felt it loving even more.

To this day I can picture his face in my mind, the boy made of stone, he still stays with me. I saw something in his eyes that I can't explain. I've seen it; I've felt it. That boy is one of the few things I regret from my trip to Ayacucho; I wished I could have had more time.

Later, I learned in my travels that a lot of these children go through sexual and physical abuse, and it happens to boys as well as girls. It's horrific beyond words.

Many more surprising things were in store for me in Ayacucho.

One night, some of us from the volunteer group decided to go out to the markets. We made our way through the stalls brimming with local produce, stacks of cheese, fruits, and vegetables spread out on woven blankets and makeshift tables. As we passed by the vendors, I noticed many of the women wore traditional outfits with skirts and shawls. Some of them would peer out from under their flat brimmed hats to look at us curiously with a smile.

I noticed that some of the girls I had seen at the day center were there working with their mothers, selling wares late into the evening. **From what I could tell, they seemed happy, laughing and running in bare feet on the soft dirt in between the stalls, selling sweets and candies.** I marveled at how each family took it in stride and were both at peace and proud of their jobs. None of the girls were pouting or giving their parents a hard time. Nobody was complaining about how poor they were, or how hard the work was, the way I imagine a child in a first-world country would be doing in this type of situation.

I thought, *Maybe that's because they have nothing to compare it with.*

That night, feeling joyous about my new friends, the work we were doing, the people we were meeting, and the aliveness of the place, I got drunk on Pisco sours. After years of abstinence from alcohol and finding an undeniable cozy place with some great company, one tasty Pisco, unfortunately, led to three or four. With a smile on my face, I stumbled back to the hostel after midnight with my new volunteer friends.

The next day at the center, I asked the staff about the girls we'd seen in the night markets. I may have sounded overly concerned. I understood that some of these folks probably had no idea about things like child labor laws that were common in countries like Canada. But surely, it wasn't right to pull a child out of school like that all the time.

One of the volunteers translated for us. They explained to me that the kids could only come for short amounts of time; it wasn't a full-time day center. **The parents would pull them out to work during the day, and it didn't matter if they were only four or five years old; everybody had to work.**

Well, at least the kids look happy, I thought.

I discovered another interesting thing. One afternoon, I noticed my jeans were starting to change color from wearing them every day, and I was running out of clean essentials, so I went up to the laundry "area" on the roof of the building. The white paint was chipped and peeling, and scraps of building materials were lying around, but it was somewhat clean up there. You had to bring your own bucket of soapy water and scrub your t-shirts and jeans and hang them to dry under the awning. It wasn't ideal, but it was the only option. Everybody did their laundry by hand, and this was definitely a new experience for me.

That day, I noticed a family living on the top of the building. Adjacent to the laundry area was a small storage room off to the side, which they had fashioned into living quarters, making it into a home. After seeing them multiple times, **I came to the conclusion that they were one of the happiest (yet poorest) families I'd seen to date.**

In the afternoon, the eldest girl would come home in her school uniform. The mother and daughter were always laughing and talking, helping each other to hang the laundry and do chores. In the center of the room was a makeshift table that was used for everything from doing homework to eating breakfast. There were no chairs that I could see, they sat on the chipped concrete floor, and used the rolled up thin mattresses pushed against the wall to sleep on at night. They had no TV; I didn't even see a fridge. But a radio was playing music. I was amazed. Even though extremely cramped and without any distractions, they never seemed to argue or get annoyed with each other.

If you looked close enough at their eyes and how they looked and addressed one another, they looked truly happy to be together. If you saw them outside of their home, you would never know they were poor as they were, and all living in one room. It was so foreign to me.

I thought, *How can they be this way? They don't even have their own space or any privacy.*

My thoughts traveled back to that enormous house I had bought in Caledon just so my friend's kids could come over and play with the "rich kids." I didn't buy it because I loved the big space—I barely knew what to do with it (besides sliding across the living room floor like Tom Cruise in *Risky Business*)—but to reward myself and prove to myself I was successful. In contrast, here was a family that had nothing, yet they were smiling and sharing time with each other like there was no better place to be in the world. It was eye-opening for me. I was starting to think that all this stuff we valued back home might be what's keeping us apart.

I began to wonder, *Why is it so easy for them, but for us, it's not?*

City of Abandoned Children

✳✳✳

We never saw the kids in the sewers, but we heard about them often.

Rumors had been circulating among the volunteers about street children who were living in the sewers underneath Ayacucho, deep underground where it was filthy. You could imagine the smell—rotting animals, feces, and the entire waste of a small town in the third world. **They would sleep in the sewer at night instead of the parks where they were at risk of getting robbed, raped, or worse.**

I never ventured into the sewers, nor did I see anyone who looked like they were sleeping in them. But I did find another unlikely safe haven for street kids: the cemetery.

In Peru, as in most South American countries, the dead are highly respected. Every month, families would go down to the local *cemeterios* to sit at the graves of their loved ones and pay their respects.

One day, the staff took us down to a large local cemetery, and I noticed that a group of children was wandering the grounds. Most of the kids had no shoes, some had sandals, and many of them had calves and feet caked with dirt. With curiosity, I watched them tagging along and following the families around. There wasn't a lot of cremation in this town, and families were commonly buried in plots, and sometimes with large stone markers. **I realized the children were organizing the flowers and cleaning off the gravestones for money.**

At times, Ayacucho, as beautiful as it was, felt like a city of abandoned children—and in a way, it was. This was in 2006, and it was hard to imagine that just a few decades prior, Peru had been rocked by political turmoil. In the 1980s, places like Ayacucho had become sites for guerilla warfare and martial law, which birthed a violent revolution. As Ayacucho's graveyards filled during this time of genocide and unrest, hundreds of children were left without parents.

That day, we befriended some of the children in the graveyard. We gave them haircuts and taught them how to manage their money and some basic etiquette, like, "Don't be too pushy when approaching families," "Be respectful," and "Say thank you." We taught them how to read basic words and they recited them back to us. I learned that they slept in certain areas of the graveyard at night and would only come out during the day. **I was in awe of these children's resourcefulness, playfulness, and willingness to learn,** but the thought of them sleeping among the gravestones bothered me, and every night when I passed by the cemetery, I felt my heart get heavy.

I did a lot of walking in Ayacucho; in fact, I'd say it was my second favorite thing to do. Every day, after dinner around 6pm, I would walk back to the hostel. I would walk as slowly as possible, taking in all the details of my surroundings and remembering the faces and smiles of the children I saw that day, until the town was pitch black. Ayacucho was somewhat situated in a valley surrounded by a mountainous, hilly region, with no real neighboring cities, and no external light to penetrate the darkness. I especially liked looking up where you could see a sky crammed full of beautiful stars as they pierced the darkness.

One night, walking back from a late dinner and taking notes, I found myself alone on a stone road when the electricity and street lights went out. In the pitch black, I had to feel my way through town by touching the sides of the buildings to figure out where I was. I've never experienced anything like it. From what I could "hear," there were no generators kicking in or secondary street lighting, nothing. I couldn't tell if someone were coming around the corner that I might bump into, or whether I was just about to fall off the street curb. I carefully shuffled along in the darkness, inch by inch, with my left hand cascading along the uneven walls, trying to keep absolutely silent to hear the slightest movement around me.

Just as I approached the area where I was staying, the power went back on. I found myself standing next to a wooden gate about ten feet high, on a narrow street with a lot of small houses. I heard trumpets warming up in the distance. Tacked onto the aged and weathered surface of the gate, which was 100 years old at least, was a hand painted sign in Spanish. I knew enough to know that it said there was a party.

Seeing some of the volunteers approaching a few doors down across the street, I motioned to them. I asked them if they knew what was going on. Nobody knew. **So, I did something totally unlike me; I raised my right hand, curled it tightly and knocked on this stranger's door.**

A few minutes later, an older woman came to the door. She peeked out, squinted her eyes at us, and then motioned enthusiastically with a wide smile for us to come inside.

I looked at the others. We shrugged our shoulders and said, "Sure, let's go!"

We descended a long set of stone steps. It was an intimidating drop down from the street, maybe 20 feet of stairs. The steps were handmade from concrete, uneven, and crafted possibly at the time of ancient civilization (I'm exaggerating), so it was slow going. There was a lot of garbage on each side of the narrow walkway, and a large fence on one side. We could hear the trumpets, drums, and laughter getting louder. I thought, *Oh my God, what did I get us into?*

When we got to the bottom, a large birthday party was in full swing. Beautifully spirited people everywhere, entire families, everyone from age 2 to 102, all enjoying themselves in an intimate courtyard. Little kids sat at the tables with the adults, and someone's *abuelita* (grandmother) walked by with a large pitcher of beer. In front of the crowd a band played folk tunes—I saw a tuba player, trumpet players, and an old three-piece drum set—and most everyone was up on their feet dancing. They cheered when they saw us, and welcomed us in. **Before I could say no, someone pulled me onto the "dancefloor."**

I'd never danced so willing or joyfully before. I was definitely the person at a party who would stand stiffly by the wall, desperately waiting for an opportunity to slip out the door unnoticed. Back then, I would judge people who were drinking excessively and find any excuse to leave unfamiliar company. But something about this party and this moment in Ayacucho was undeniable. I was up dancing and having a great time. It was an awakening.

On the dance floor, someone handed me a cup of alcohol, scooped out of what looked like a recycled drum (maybe they saw my dancing and felt I needed it). I decided to go with the moment. I took a swig of it and hoped I wouldn't wake up blind.

Everywhere I looked I saw generation after generation celebrating. Parents passing pitchers of beer around, little kids dancing and holding hands. Some of the local men were flirting with the female volunteers from the UK, and vice versa, some of the Peruvian girls were flirting with the male volunteers. Nothing aggressive or dramatic, all in good fun. If I had to sum it up, I'd say that nobody was worried about tomorrow; **they were just happy being alive and, more importantly, together in this moment.**

Coming from a seemingly perfect life—where I had to buy something new just to feel important and alive—I realized how sterile our social gatherings back home were in comparison. Everyone played at a safe distance, we never got in depth or connected on a meaningful level about anything. There was always an intellectual discussion among friends; we'd share knowledge or trade opinions about popular topics of interest, but never anything that showed true vulnerability or touched on what brought us genuine joy. To be honest, we appeared to be more affectionate with our pets than with other human beings and even our own families at times.

I wondered, *Why was it so difficult for us to make those connections?*

Most of us we were spending our days working, saving, growing, and chasing money and success all at the expense of our families and our own sense of connectedness and fulfillment. We were missing out on a lot of experiences along the way, the simple joys. And here were people who didn't have even one percent of the material things we had, yet they were full, alive, and joyful.

What did we really have in Canada that they didn't have in South America? We had allergies (which are more uncommon in Latin America), an abundance of stress, unhappiness, bullying, and anxiety disorders. **All these things we suffered with or worked hard for back home, it all seemed so superfluous to me in that moment.**

Of course, we were better off in some ways, but not in others. And the ways in which we thought we had it better, most of them were visions of reality made up in our minds and from our popular culture and not in tune with what's really important.

I looked around at the relaxed and genuine faces of the families around me, and I recalled a line from a movie where Winnie the Pooh said something like, "Yesterday was so exhausting when it was today." I realized, even more, that you couldn't get that kind of happiness by worrying about a tomorrow that isn't there yet.

At home, I was constantly thinking, doing, and building. I always thought, *Sure I make a decent income, but what if I could make another $100,000, $200,000, or $500,000 more?* Here in Peru, my only thought was of the girls and their laughter with their mothers in the night market, being grateful to spend time with the volunteers, and my "boy made of stone." I thought of these things and my heart was full of the purest and simplest of emotions. I felt alive. In that moment, the regret of yesterday and the worries of tomorrow had no place. Without all that noise in my head, I was able to see so many things I didn't see before. I went from the pitch darkness to a birthday party where people were enjoying themselves and the abundance of a material-less life, not sitting and judging each other. I saw the pigeons in the square, not worrying about my bank account. I saw a child sweeping fallen leaves off a gravestone, watching the miracle of his smile as he performed the simplest of tasks for a stranger.

Every usually stiff muscle in my body was at ease. **Who needs anything more than this moment?**

The band began to increase their intensity and apparently struck a favorite tune, and even the most exhausted revelers jumped to their feet. I took another sip of the home-brewed "whatever" in my mangled plastic cup and joined in the fun. I had to laugh. It was so simple! I had come all this way, thousands of miles to South America, just to figure out that all I needed was to slow down, "stop and smell the wild flowers."

I had to witness, not with my head, but experience it in my heart, what was always right there dancing in the "mirror of life" in front of me.

There were miracles happening around me all along. I didn't have to go far to find them, I just had to get out of my own way.

Machu Picchu
No Turning Back – Unless a Donkey...
✳✳✳

I glanced up ahead of me on the trail and wondered how much further we had to go. My heart felt as if it were going to explode and my calves were on fire, but I couldn't risk stopping. I put my head down and kept walking.

At this point, I had fallen so far behind my hiking group, that only one lone Polish girl was behind me. Every time I heard the swish of her overstuffed blue backpack gaining on me, I sped up. I thought, *There's no way I'm going to be the last person; she's not passing me.* She was my secret motivation, and I secretly thanked her for it.

After leaving Ayacucho, I decided to take some more time to be with myself and, more importantly, to reflect on what I was uncovering and what I had already uncovered. I decided to end my trip by hiking Machu Picchu. **Looking back, I laugh at myself, thinking,** *If I only knew...*

Even if I had been a seasoned hiker (which I wasn't), it would have been a monumental accomplishment. Marathons are more consistent. The entire trail was only 40 kilometers, but you had start at 9,000 feet above sea level and go up and down the whole time. Down 1,000 feet and back up to 13,000 feet to Dead Woman's Pass. The next major point was down 3,000 feet, back up to 13,776 feet, and back down to 12,000 feet, and all the way to 4,000 ft down to Machu Picchu. You could be at a flat plateau for an hour and then find yourself going straight up a mountain again. It was grueling, physically and mentally.

All the rest of my group were seasoned hikers, even the youngest of them; it was humbling and welcome test. It took us four days total, twelve hours of hiking each day, and each hike was well beyond my believed physical capabilities. We'd be climbing a mountain for what felt like hours and suddenly be in the clouds. **Halfway through, my heart was throbbing in pain, my lungs labored in the high altitude, and my legs felt like they weighed a ton.** But I had no choice; I had to keep going. Unless something dire happened—in which case, a guide would take you back on a donkey—the only way out of it was forward.

One good thing was that most of the walking was done in isolation, and I had a lot of time to think. That was a good and bad thing. I played a lot of upbeat music like *Coldplay* and *U2* when we were going down, but I had to listen to something harder and more industrial like *Rammstein* and the *Red Hot Chili Peppers* going up to motivate me. In between, I had many moments of daydreaming about my girlfriend Diana in Toronto, how amazing she was, and the times we had shared, anything to keep my mind off the pain.

There were no showers on the trail, but by day two, we found a stream and were able to wash our feet and socks. Most of us had blisters of one kind or another. None of us really worried about how we smelled; it wasn't a concern. At night, we'd camp on the plateaus. The *sherpas* (guides) would expertly assemble our tents and then cook us a gourmet meal. The food was outstanding. They'd serve us six- and seven-course meals, big platters of meat, vegetables, and fish, and bake entire cakes with icing and everything on the campfire. After our feast, they paired us up in small tents to sleep for the night.

The last day, in Aguas Calientes, a few hours from Machu Picchu we woke up around 4am, had breakfast, and packed up in the dark. We had to get an early start up the mountain if we wanted to get there before the crowds and the clouds moved in. I remember the last bit of the trail was treacherous and narrow, and we were warned the llamas could be kind of aggressive. So, every time we saw them coming toward us, we had to quickly find a safe place to stand. It took us several hours of steady hiking to get to Machu Picchu, and I was simultaneously laughing and angry the whole time because buses kept passing us, and I realized I had put myself through all this last stretch of agony *for what?*

When we finally reached Machu Picchu, it was like heaven. The peacefulness, the purity of the air, and the energy was unbelievable up there. I didn't want to leave. Many in our group had a moment of wondering what it would be like to stay overnight. It was definitely my favorite of the "wonders of the world," and I've had the luxury to see four of them.

A young lady from Japan in our group was clearly the best photographer. When we got back down the mountain, she shared her photos with everyone. All of us created great friendships on the trip. An outgoing guy from Australia was always good for a laugh along the trail. A guy from Montreal who owned a cafe had an intellectual insight into everything. A couple from California who had both recently divorced were finding themselves together. A German who was morose and always making these gloomy statements that started with, "Yeah, well…" But we managed to get a few laughs out of him once in a while.

After Machu Picchu, I stayed a few nights in Cusco to take a look around the area and do some sightseeing. Afterwards, I would fly back to Lima, and from there, on to Santiago, Chile.

I had been emailing Diana from the Internet cafes when I could find one. I would update her and share with her what I was uncovering. She was also helping me make a few arrangements before arriving in the next city. My plan was to cross as much of the South American continent as possible and work with as many children and interview as many organizations and nonprofits as I could during this time. Diana had worked with Red Cross in Colombia, so she understood the organizations I was looking to volunteer with and was writing to the places where I might visit. We both agreed that the best place to go after Peru was Chile, because it was just south, only a three-and-a-half-hour flight.

As I laid my battered and exhausted body down on the hotel bed my last night in Cusco, I marveled at my ability to be adaptable despite the "terrain." Earlier that day I was scrambling up the steep cliffs of Machu Picchu in the rain, clinging desperately to brush and whatever else I could grab onto. **Sometimes, life was like that—a messy, beautiful adventure.** I wondered what insights, tests, and adventures would be waiting for me in Chile. After a little taste of Peru, my sense of purpose and courage had only grown stronger.

Before I lost consciousness in my sleep, I had a thought: *Isn't it amazing what we can accomplish when there's no turning back?*

Chile:
Beauty is
Beyond the 1%

May 2006
Santiago, Chile
***

W hen I eventually arrived in Santiago, I understood why I needed to serve in Peru first. Santiago is the capital of Chile, and it definitely lived up to its reputation for being one of the largest and fastest growing economies in Latin America. I could feel the excitement as we flew over the sophisticated city with winding freeways and high-rises on the skyline. The background of the city was surrounded by an intimidating mountain range with snow-covered peaks. **Some of the more developed areas even looked similar to parts of Toronto.**

Coming to Santiago after being in such a small community in Peru was quite a jolt to my senses; it felt like I had been living in the countryside my whole life and finally arrived in the "big city."

Exiting the airport, I flagged down a taxi and was relieved to see the inside of the cab was somewhat normal. I say that because some of the taxis in Ayacucho, Peru were hardly fit for the road. I remember one time in the passenger side, looking down between my legs to see a big milk jug of gasoline with a plastic tube that went from under the dash and syphoned gas to the fuel tank. Being in a regular car with proper flooring (and the gas tank in the back where it should be) was quite reassuring.

Thinking back on my time in Ayacucho, I realized going there first was just what I needed. Coming from Canada to an uncluttered, simpler way of life where 90% of the things I had been worrying about were less of a priority, was the perfect palate cleanser for the rest of my trip. If I'd gone straight to Chile first, it would have been too similar. **My childhood, my upbringing, my opinions, my concerns, I had to learn to let some of these limiting perspectives go to see anew.**

It's like the analogy of getting a new car.

Remember buying your first new car, how exciting it was? However, times change and the efficiency and the adaptive technology of the vehicles we drive are constantly improving. So, when we can afford to, we buy new cars. But some people love hanging onto their older cars, even for decades. It's like taking that 1975 Chevelle out on the freeway—the world around us has changed, but we haven't—and everyone is passing us by. What happens when our lives change, or our destination changes? Will that car built 50 years ago still perform?

The world is always evolving, and just like buying a new car, from time to time, we have to refresh the way we look at the world. I've learned over time that it's healthy and important to challenge views we held in the past and see if they still serve us *and* the greater good today. Thankfully, Peru definitely did that for me.

Before I checked into the new hostel, I decided to find something to eat. I was really looking forward to going to a restaurant and being able to order something familiar off the menu. My last meal in Peru was chicken soup, it was .50 cents for a big bowl, and when I went to stir it, the chicken's foot came out! It was a bit shocking; this pale knobly thing with claws just bubbled up and then went back into the bowl. To say some of the food in Ayacucho was "authentic" would be an understatement.

At this point, I was craving Japanese food. After driving around Santiago for about an hour in a taxi, I saw a sign for a *Benihana Japanese restaurant*, of all places.

"Stop the car," I told the driver.

I paid the fare and went inside a large shopping center where the restaurant was located. I was greeted by the hostess and immediately seated at a table on the patio. I set my enormous red backpack on the floor next to me, and eagerly opened the menu.

Like a man who had been wandering in the wilderness, I was ready to spend a few bucks just to enjoy a familiar dish from home. Everything was extremely expensive. Each dish was $30 or $40 dollars. That was a lot back then, even for Chile. For the next hour, I ate like a king, dish after dish of appetizers, sushi, and *teppanyaki*; **I spared no expense. I told myself, "I deserve this! I'm treating myself."**

After my feast, I took a stroll around the shopping center. I went into the Apple store, looked through a few clothing shops, and had a fresh juice. It was good to be around familiar settings. After filling my eyes and stomach with all this distraction, my feet were beginning to feel a bit tired and I decided it was time to head over to the hostel. Unlike the place I stayed at in Peru (with no electricity or hot water), this would be the very first hostel with basic amenities I'd ever been to.

When I arrived at the hostel, I was greeted by two friendly faces. I stood at the front desk and took it all in. The energy was different than what I was used to. Foreign people were everywhere but for varying reasons, and lots of communal spaces were available where people could sit and talk and share their experiences. The lady checking me in informed me I had the option to take a private room, but I declined. Despite my lavish lunch, I still wanted to be as congruent with the journey as possible and do my best to stay grounded. I wanted the full experience.

The full experience turned out to be a shared room with six other people in it, both guys and gals. *It's co-ed, great,* I thought. That was definitely something new and different. The bedroom was quite small, so I chose the second last available bed close to the door, sat my stuff down, locked my valuables away, and went to the common area to mingle with my fellow travelers. I quickly realized I was one of the older ones there at age 31, but I didn't feel uncomfortable; I was just "aware" of it.

Over the next few days, I would get to know my new roommates quite well. One was a heavier guy who was outspoken, and a few ladies who were "partners" were very vocal as well. I also met a guy from Ireland who was a colorful character, as he had a lot of opinions and shared them as loudly as possible. He had a fun energy, but he also seemed like the type of person who could be understanding, someone you could have a good chat with. He had a smile that made you feel he was genuine.

I walked around the hostel to get a better look at the amenities. It was functional, with a very basic kitchen and some helpers around to keep things tidy. The showers were very amusing. The stalls were narrow and didn't really leave much room to move around in, but I was relieved it was better than the "hose and bucket" situation in Peru. On my way out, I passed a "cute" maid in the hallway; she glanced at me in an engaging way and smiled.

The next day, I decided to do some exploring around Santiago before starting my work with the children. I didn't feel like carrying my stuff around the city, so I bought a lock from the gift shop and bolted my backpack to the bed. It was generally understood that you had to lock everything down, especially your bags, as things did get stolen at times. I left the hostel early and headed to the downtown area, the part of the city where it seemed easiest to discover something new and do some people watching.

I saw an unusual amount of shows in the streets of downtown, performers, puppets for the kids, magic shows, and a lot of artistic expression everywhere. I passed by an entire eight-piece band playing on the street dressed to the nines with red suit jackets, and people dancing in the street. **Whether it was someone with intricate tattoos, or a person wearing a stylish hat and boots, the Chileans held their own.** It was extremely colorful. Portrait painters and performers on the street corners, a boy dancing with a drum on his back, stilt walkers strolling through the avenues—that was their everyday thing.

That afternoon I took as many photos as I could of people's faces, I was trying to capture moments like these when they were just being themselves. I'm sure I could have gone into other areas of the city and found the worst. Every once in a while, I would see a sign about child trafficking hanging in a shop window and other little warnings like these, but, at that moment, I chose to find these joyful street scenes instead.

Then I saw something I'd never witnessed in any other country before.

I was in Bicentenario Park walking along the edge near the river, enjoying the sweeping panoramic views of the city. Across from me on the opposite bank were some artists on the grass selling their wares on blankets about four or five blocks long, laden with handmade crafts and jewelry. Suddenly, three to four massive green military cargo trucks pulled up in a row, and dozens of government soldiers ran out. Everybody darted, frantically trying to wrap up their makeshift shops. This wasn't just a warning; the government meant business, and it was apparent they were chasing the vendors down like fugitives.

The scene went from peaceful to confrontational in a matter of seconds. Some of the vendors stood defiantly at a distance with an "us against them" attitude—straight backs, lowered brows, chins jutting out—as the Chilean soldiers in berets gathered up their goods and raced them back to the trucks. I almost got the sense that if the government wasn't so militant about enforcing the laws, I could see the vendors fighting back. I wouldn't be surprised if they did. Some of these folks carried themselves in that manner, you got the sense that they weren't necessarily violent, but they would stand up for what they believed in. As artists and vendors, they were strong-willed people, as much as they were trying to make a living.

In Peru you would sometimes see a military presence in certain areas, but I never felt any sense of insecurity from the police or military. This was the first time I'd experienced anything like this, and I found myself leaving the park hastily that day.

It occurred to me that I was largely ignorant of the social situation in Chile. After what I saw in Bicentenario Park, **I decided to keep my head down and focus on my mission and purpose for this trip: the children.**

Hogar de Cristo
April 2006

***

"Your need for acceptance can make you invisible
in this world. Don't let anything stand in the way
of the light that shines through this form.
Risk being seen in all of your glory."
—Jim Carrey

My first organization there was called *Hogar de Cristo*, the "Home of Christ" a charity started in 1944 by a Jesuit priest. This was the largest public charity in Chile serving over 25,000 people in extreme poverty. **After corresponding with them via email, I had successfully arranged interviews with several of the directors at the organization.** It was a two-part plan: interview the directors of the foundation and learn more about their programs, as well as their successes, and unique challenges, and invest the remaining majority of my time with the children, to learn more about what determines a better quality of life for them.

As I arrived at *Hogar de Cristo* and exited the taxi, the staff and the interpreter came out and enthusiastically greeted me at the front gate. After shaking their hands, we walked over to one of the main buildings. My knowledge of Spanish was growing, but I still had to rely on the interpreter. What I understood from him, was that we'd be visiting the orphanage first.

Chile seemed so full of surprises; again, as always, I wasn't sure what to expect.

Inside the building looked like a cross between an old school and a hospital. Our sneakers softly squeaked on the ceramic floors as we went down the wide hallway. Similar to a clinic, the walls were painted solid pastel colors, with charts of the day's activities, down to the minute, hanging on them. There wasn't a lot of life in the décor, everything was basic, yet functional.

One staff member motioned for us to follow her to another building; she said something in Spanish that I didn't quite catch. I looked to the translator for an explanation.

"We're going to go visit the newborns first," he said.

As we approached the door, the interpreter explained to me that this part of the orphanage was for babies whose mothers couldn't take care of them and dropped them off late at night, abandoned them in the hospital, or worse. Entering the building, the children's cries seemed to ring down the crumbling powder blue concrete walls. After passing a few empty rooms filled with bare metal cots, I approached the room holding the babies.

Despite all my experiences, living in foster care, being abandoned, living with drug dealers and in parks, and even after working with over a hundred children in Peru, nothing could have prepared me for what I saw next.

Standing in front of a tall white door at the end of the hallway, I peered through a circular portal (like a window on a ship) to look inside the room. On the floor, were about 20 babies, lying on their backs, side by side, with just one caregiver overseeing the babies from the corner of the room. As I gasped, my hand flew to my mouth, trying to catch my breath. I had to quickly turn around. I stood there for a few seconds. The emotions were too much, I needed to cry.

I never thought it would hit me so hard. Not because they were babies, necessarily. I didn't have children at this point; I wasn't even particularly close with my friends' kids either. I knew babies were a special gift, but so were a lot of other things. From what I could tell, they were in a clean room with a decent mat to lie on, and they appeared healthy. Some had big bellies and chubby faces, and others had bottles in their hands.

What really struck me was seeing those big eyes looking up at me crying, pleading for attention. Instantly, a flood of memories and the feelings I had of being abandoned as a child came to me. It was a visceral feeling. **All these children on their backs were looking for someone to pick them up; it tore me apart.** *How painful.* The intensity of what was going on in the room on an emotional level was too much for me to handle.

Thinking back to all the violence and trauma I experienced growing up, I had to learn how to control the emotions and the meaning of the situation. I remembered when my mother was raped and ran into our apartment crying and screaming, seeing a gun for the first time in a "drug house," and watching my parents fight and being slammed into the walls. Yes, at times, I was scared for my life, but, somehow, I learned how to deal with it. Honestly, did I have a choice?

For some reason this was different; I couldn't control my reaction. You could have cut off my arm and I wouldn't have felt as much pain as I felt in that moment. It started in my chest, filled my shoulders, then my neck and head, and finally back down to my legs. It was a shaking, painful weakness that made my body feel hopeless in that moment.

A quote from Mother Theresa came to mind. "We think sometimes that poverty is only being hungry, naked and homeless. **The poverty of being unwanted, unloved and uncared for is the greatest poverty."**

Even though these children had staff there doing the best they could do, it still struck me like a nail in the heart. *How painful their hearts must feel! How many of them will grow up thinking they were unloved?*

When I had regained control of myself, I went inside. I was able to walk around inside the room, but they didn't let me pick up any of the babies (I obeyed, even though my heart told me not to). After that, I was taken to another room with somewhat older children. I understood that the staff were just trying to show me what they were dealing with and, at the same time, how well structured the programs were.

Next, we went into the recreation room, it was somewhat crudely constructed, maybe 800 square feet, with small round tables, a few recycled couches, and a TV. Caregivers were on duty, attending to the children, most of whom were between two and four years old, some still feeding from bottles and others crawling around in diapers.

"These are also orphans without parents," the interpreter explained. "They get fed and taken care of during the day by the *Hogar* staff."

My first instinct was to play with all of them. I didn't want to give them a speech, and say, "Hello, I'm from Canada." I didn't want to tell them everything was going to be okay or try to help them in any way. Their basic needs were already being met by the institution around them. What I really wanted to do was just be with them, stay with them in this moment, and appreciate them for who they were.

Somehow, I wanted to transmit this message to them, "Let's be silly if you want to be silly. If you're serious, let's be serious. But let's not try to fix you, because you're already enough."

Soon, my focus turned to a brother and sister who were playing together. I sat at a table near them and joined the fun. The little girl was quite active, running around the table, giggling, making faces at me. They weren't shy at all, and they spoke to me in Spanish, without exhaustion. It was really funny because I would speak English back to them and they didn't seem to mind or care that neither of us could understand. As we were about to go, I stood up, and the little boy wrapped his arms around my leg and wouldn't let me go.

It was tough. I had just been through the baby situation, and now this little boy wouldn't let go of my leg. I looked down at his big brown eyes and thought, *How do I adopt one of these children?*

I had to remind myself that I had a purpose, and I had to keep going. Adopting one or two of the kids wouldn't have been the solution. But it was hard.

A caregiver came up and asked me to help feed the children before I left. I said "*SI*," and, within seconds, was holding a toddler with worried eyes. Honestly, he had every right to be worried, as I did such a bad job. This was the first time I'd ever held a baby in my arms, let alone try to feed one with a bottle. My attempt was a mess. Milk spilled all over his shirt (and mine). Thankfully, he was very patient with me as I managed to get most of his breakfast into his belly.

As I held him, I noticed he had this "mustache" of medicinal paste under his nose and sores around his nostrils. He had some sort of cold. Also, he was heavy and probably a little too old to be bottle fed, but I didn't mind. In that brief moment in time, all that mattered was him. Not the Porsche, not my new company, not what other people thought of me. I didn't feel the need to take a "selfie" or run and tell my friends, "Hey! I fed a young orphan boy today." **The moment was only important to the two of us.**

At the end of the day, I sat down with some of the directors to ask them what their greatest challenges (and successes) were and took more studious notes. After the meetings, I thanked the staff and the translator for taking the time to show me around, and I told them I was looking forward to seeing them again in the morning.

As I left that day, I reflected on what I'd just experienced. I thought *Hogar* was going to be easy, that I was going to just go in there and be able to look at things with a more clinical outlook. The first part of my plan was to meet the directors, tour the facility, find out more about their structure and funding, and I felt like I'd succeeded in that. I learned that they raised and managed funds for the betterment of all their programs, and it was very well organized with 500 projects across Chile. When asking questions of the directors, I found them to be totally transparent; they were tolerant of my inquiries and very congruent.

But my entire plan got thrown out the window the second I encountered the children. I couldn't reconcile the "process" with their "needs" in my head exactly; so, instead, I went in there raw and open, as if I were seeing children like that for the first time and learning anew what I thought I already understood. Admittedly, I was still figuring it all out.

That night, I couldn't wait to get back to the hostel; I wanted to reach out to Diana and share all the things I'd seen and learned that day with her. I wanted to tell her how all the kids had such unique personalities, and that I'd held a little boy and wished I could adopt him. And I wanted to tell her I was missing her deeply.

The Insight that Backfired

***

Whenever I left *Hogar*, I always made a point to walk back to the hostel to give myself time to reflect on the events of the day and discover new neighborhoods, people, and experiences.

Time had always slowed down for me after a day with the children. As I walked back, I noticed every step, every crack in the sidewalk. I'd consciously notice my pace and walk with a fullness and presence of my surroundings never experienced back home. *What else can I see that I haven't seen before?* I must have looked like a weirdo, but I didn't care. I just had to worry about being in the moment with my surroundings, not work, nor material stuff. I didn't worry about who was going to keep me up at night in the crowded room, or what I was going to eat later. I chose not to worry about any of it; I was too full of what was happening in the moment.

I'd also look at people's faces and wonder what they might have looked and lived like as a child. I spent all day being so present with these children that I was starting to look at people and started to uncover an essence about them that was so alive as a child, yet suppressed today. Although I had the best of intentions, this close observation and admiration of people didn't always go as planned.

One late afternoon I was headed back to the hostel after a long day of working with the kids at *Hogar*. It was around 6pm and I had a three hour walk to get back to the hostel. I should get there just before it got dark. About an hour into my walk, I saw two ladies up ahead on the road and decided to test out my new "awareness tool."

I made eye contact and smiled at them as they approached.

Then something strange happened. They sort of slowed down, and then came to a standstill just as I passed. *That's odd,* I thought. I turned around less than ten seconds later and realized, *These aren't women.*

The moment I thought this, they turned around and started following me.

The hair on my arms stood up; I instinctively started walking faster.

Nothing like this had ever happened to me before. Of course, we had the LGBTQ community in Canada, but it was far from being prominent the way it was in South America back then, and, more importantly, the energy of the situation, regardless of gender, was concerning. So, this was a bit new for me. I didn't know what to do. I started making random left and right turns, glancing over my shoulder to see if they were still following me. *Yep,* they were still there.

I walked faster, and they walked faster.

So, I slowed down hoping they would pass me, but they slowed down, too.

I was starting to get extremely uncomfortable.

I didn't have a GPS or a map on my phone, so I was all on my own. If I turned down the wrong street, I knew I was in big trouble. All I had was a paper map, and nothing says "Hello, I'm a tourist" quite like a paper map. There were a lot of factors going on, I had to shake these people, but if I made too many turns, I could also wind up lost, or in a situation where I was boxed in. Santiago, like most other big cities, had its bad neighborhoods. The last thing I wanted was to be stuck in one.

After about ten minutes of this cat and mouse game, I ducked into an Italian restaurant and hid behind a group of people standing in the entrance. I watched the window eagerly, waiting for them to pass by so I could make sure they were gone before I went back out. After a minute or two, I gave up and decided instead, to lay low and have some pasta.

From now on, I had to be mindful and a little less "friendly" with my smile toward strangers.

I was exhausted by the time I got back to the hostel. The next day was a critical day, *Hogar* wanted to have some meetings with me so I could learn more about their programs. I was intrigued where the donations were coming from and how supportive the government was. Unlike other organizations I'd visited, they never once complained about government support; it always seemed very positive.

Also, something very special was happening. They had invited me to see two outside projects, a sort of outreach program where the *Hogar* staff were helping the homeless and working to transition them out of living on the streets and into co-op housing. A lot of these were homeless families with children living on the streets of Chile. I was really excited for this, as it fit in with my mission to see children in as many different living situations as I could, in order to find the answer to my question: what was that one thing that could make life better for them?

It was reassuring to know that even in the darkest situations, someone was always out there to give these families some help and get them out of their situation. I was respectful and in awe of that.

The Beautiful Couple in the Landfill
***

"True Happiness is experienced privately, temporary happiness is displayed publicly."
— *Erik Kikuchi*

It was late at night, around 10pm, when the *Hogar* staff picked me up. I climbed inside the compact Japanese van and squeezed in between two caseworkers in the darkness of the very last row of seats. I had to sit with my knees glued together and my elbows tucked in so we could all fit inside. After about an hour drive, every few minutes the van would stop, and we would get out and talk to people on the street. A routine evening ended up being far much more.

Finally, the van stopped. I squinted out the back window and saw what looked like mounds of trash and large machinery, it appeared to be a recycling center. I turned to the translator and asked him to confirm.

One of the caseworkers nodded. "It's a landfill and recycling center," the translator said.

Okay, this should be interesting, I thought.

We crawled out of the van, ducking our heads to avoid banging them on the door frame, and stood up to stretch our cramped limbs. The first thing I noticed were some figures in the distance, men and women opening up trash bags, inspecting the contents, and closing them in an orderly fashion. From time to time an item would be removed and set aside. I was impressed by how respectful they were of the environment around them; they weren't leaving trash all over.

In Chile, trash picking, among those living on the street, wasn't uncommon. Every night, hundreds of people would work from 10pm until 5am, combing the streets, going through garbage cans looking for paper, aluminum, and cardboard. They would haul the recyclables out in rickshaws made out of things like wood and bicycle tires, carried them out on their backs in bundles or rolled them on dollies fashioned with makeshift wheels. **You would often see entire families trash picking, a husband and wife usually, or a parent and a child.** I was told that the children would sleep during the day, wherever they were squatting. Then, at night they would accompany their parents on their rounds through the dark streets of the city. For these families, it was the only way they could make money.

The caseworkers explained that there was an unspoken agreement between many residences and businesses regarding the folks sorting through their garbage. They were mindful of the trash pickers. Most of the time, they were careful not to mix food or dirty diapers or tissues in with their recyclables, and they wrapped broken glass carefully. They did their best to help these people find what they needed when they were sorting through the garbage. **Even though the situation was less than desirable, I found this little bit of human compassion heartening.**

The caseworkers were walking around the trash mounds with clipboards and file folders, talking to people sorting and collecting. I sensed that we were there also looking for someone specific.

Soon after, a husband and wife emerged from the piles of trash and approached us. They had a baby stroller, a basic thing made out of pink plastic that they'd found in the garbage somewhere. Sleeping inside was a small child. The first thing I noticed as they came close and greeted us was the man's big smile—he looked genuinely happy.

They were small in stature, almost young, adultlike. From outward appearances, they didn't seem deprived or depressed at all, but you could tell they were living on the streets by the condition of their clothes and shoes. The wife didn't seem distraught by their situation at all, even though it was so late. I was intrigued by their contentedness and lack of any shame or concern. After the caseworkers did their check in, and with the help of the interpreter, I warmly began asking questions about their background.

They shared with me that they'd met when they were teenagers and fell in love; they'd been together and on the streets since the age of fourteen. **You could see by their glances and the shared joy in their eyes as they told their story that they really were in love.** I had a pang of jealousy, thinking about my recent separation from my wife. They never once said things like, "It's so awful," or complained about their situation, each other, or even the government. Instead they were telling me about how much they loved each other and how much they accomplished together.

It was truly inspirational. I reflected on all the times in my past, how I complained about trivial things, and none of that could compare with what this couple was going through. We always said our marriage was a struggle, but it was nothing like what this husband and wife had to deal with: combing the streets every night, looking for garbage and recycling while caring for and protecting their baby.

I thought, *There is some truth to the saying that one man's problem is another man's treasure.*

The baby slept quietly while we talked. The wife gently rocked the child, rolling the stroller back and forth on its wheels. I asked her about her son, and her face immediately brightened. She told me they were working so hard to save up money for a co-op house so he could grow up in a safer environment and go to school.

I said, "How much do you need to save up?"

The woman paused and looked at her husband. "Two hundred and fifty dollars," they said.

"How close are you?"

They smiled, looking quite proud of themselves. "Eighty dollars."

Great, they saved eighty dollars already! I thought. My heart was soaring for them; I was so happy that they would have a home very soon.

"That's great, I know you'll get there!"

"Well, we saved eighty," the husband explained, "but we had to spend fifty dollars because our baby got pneumonia, so we're down to thirty dollars, but we'll make it back... and more..."

He said it very matter-of-factly, and, again, they didn't complain. He was just stating how it was.

Suddenly, I had a thought. I asked them, "How long did it take you to save eighty dollars?"

"Five years," he said softly.

My heart dropped. I thought, *At that rate, it would take them over ten years to get the total saved.* I felt my energy change and suddenly my focus shifted from them to myself. I felt utterly selfish and disgusted, I had just spent at *Benihana* what it took them five years to earn, without even blinking an eye. I stood there trying to contain myself.

I could see how proud they were that they'd spent most of their savings on their son. I felt cognitive dissonance. In my model of the world, everything about this was wrong. **Yet, everything was right in the way they approached it.** They didn't make things worse than they had to be, this was simply what they had to do, and it was part of their purpose. At the same time, I knew it was unjust. Such good-hearted people having to dig through garbage all night—dirty, filthy, dangerous work—for years to save an amount of money that someone could spend in less than an hour just down the street.

The contrast of two different worlds jolted me.

The reality of what other people go through with such pride and dignity hit me. I had no frame of reference for earning so little over such a long time. But I could still remember what it was like to struggle.

This couple's story reminded me of a time eleven years prior when my wife and I had nothing but each other. Andrea and I had just moved from a small town of seven thousand people to Toronto, Ontario, a city of over three million. Our place was a tiny 350 square foot basement apartment in the house of a kind and soft-spoken Indian family. The home was small, simple, and somewhat clean. Every evening, the air was always filled with the delicious smell of Indian food and loud chatter from above. At night, there would be moments lying in bed when we could hear mice rustle above us in the ceiling. My wife and I would laugh in fright, we were just happy being together.

In that very basement apartment, one night after coming home from the late shift, I watched a TV show that featured a successful young man at thirty years of age, who had reached $1.1 million in sales with his company. This was a *60-Minutes* style show on rising Canadian business owners that showcased different entrepreneurs. I'm not one hundred percent sure if his company was generating $1.1 million in sales or if he was earning that amount, but the impression was that this man had broken through. He didn't have to report to a boss, he called his own shots, he was successful and abundantly happy.

In the episode, the camera followed him around as he showed us his picture-perfect life, a wife, kids, and a beautiful home. Not only was his business thriving, his family had all the material comforts you could want from a growing and profitable business. I was hooked. I knew I was worthy and capable of accomplishing the same thing in my own life. Right then and there, I decided I was going to do whatever it would take over the next decade to make it all happen.

Eleven years later I had achieved everything I saw in that episode and more, yet it had all seemingly dissipated in a matter of months. With this deep feeling of dissatisfaction, I went looking for a different type of inspiration, one that had nothing to do with material items or wealth; it had to do with heart. I know that real inspiration should be a pull, not a push, because when it's just for ourselves, it's usually short-lived. Also, inspiration can come from surprising places. Now, I was in Chile standing in front of a landfill in Chile, talking to what seemed like a modern-day Mary and Joseph. **It struck me that I'd taken a lot for granted this whole time.** The sheer decadence of my life, blowing my money for short moments of pleasure all because I felt I deserved it, felt meaningless, yet I somehow knew it all along.

The couple went back to work, I stood by the van and watched them meticulously sorting through the bags, carefully placing the items of value in a bag. From time to time, the mother would lean down and touch the head of her sleeping child.

If I were looking for problems, I could have said, "These people shouldn't have their child out so late at night" or "Why isn't the government helping them?"

Instead, I was utterly inspired by them, and I was ashamed. To this day, they're among the strongest and most influential people I met in Chile. I honored them tremendously.

Part of me wanted to put them on a plane and take them home with me. I wanted to reach into my pocket and hand them $250. I refrained, because I knew it wasn't a solution. Instead, I focused on the miracle of who they were, and I thought, *Maybe instead of us trying to help them, perhaps we had more to learn **from** them about how to be resourceful.*

In light of that "filter," I saw them for what they truly were: a gift for many of us.

María, More Than What Others Have Labeled You

***

It was 11:30pm, on day five of my trip. We had already had a long night. My legs were beginning to cramp up again, sitting in the back of the very same micro van, and I began to wonder who we were about to meet next as we left the landfill on our way to serve the next homeless family.

As we approached our next stop, my translator turned around and said, "We're almost there, Erik. Now remember what the people at the organization told you. **This lady is different; she's not like the others we met this past week.** She has three children, but really doesn't have the mental capabilities to care for them."

He searched for the right word. "She is *mentally unstable*—I believe is the right term."

Keeping my comments to myself, I leaned back in my seat and began to remember the time when my mother and I lived in the house with drug dealers. This was after we'd moved out of the motels and parks where we'd been living in a tent, so it was a slight improvement. It was common for the guys to tell me bad things about my mother when she left to do whatever she did that day. Even though I was only 8-years-old, I had the intelligence to see and judge for myself where this information was coming from.

It used to make me so mad. I knew that if my mother had heard the things they said about her behind her back, she would have been furious. *Who did they think they were?* They hadn't seen all the hard decisions she had to make at such an early age with two young boys. How could anyone label her after knowing her for two days vs. the 9,125 other days of her life that she had already lived, experienced, and grown as a woman? More importantly, did my mother even know about this label they put on her?

My heart went out to this woman we were about to meet. Whoever she was, I promised myself that I wouldn't label her. I wouldn't judge her the way people used to judge my mother, only seeing less than 1% of who my mom really was.

We arrived at our destination, which turned out to be a seemingly small parkette, probably no more than 1,000 square feet. wide. They stopped the van on the right-hand side and pulled the doors open so the caseworkers and I could get out and stretch. **About twenty feet away, I could see the silhouette of a small female figure tending a fire inside a steel oil drum.** From time to time, she added more wood to the fire, holding her hands over the flames to keep warm. As I crawled out of the van, I also began to notice her tiny so-called "dwelling" off to the side, which appeared to be made of scraps of wood, corrugated plastic, sheet metal, and a lot of odds and ends. Then I saw a little person behind her, standing to the left about six or eight feet away. One of her children.

All of this was on a small piece of land surrounded by streets, on a patch of uneven grass and weeds, tucked under an overpass. Surprisingly enough, it was in one of the safer areas we'd seen on this mission.

We all started to walk toward her.

"Now remember, Erik, if she seems a bit different, off, or strange, it's because she has a mental disability. So just be mindful as you approach her." the translator said.

I kept thinking to myself, *Didn't he just tell me this?* Either there's a real problem with her, or they're just trying to prepare me for something out of the ordinary. I knew they meant well, but shouldn't they be more mindful of what they say?

I could have easily pictured a crazy-haired lady talking to herself or a troll-like creature under a bridge, but, instead, I found a beautiful, quiet, subdued woman standing there. I was pleasantly surprised. **I had to stand there for a moment and both witness and take it in.** She wasn't anything at all like what I would have pictured. She smiled timidly when she saw us approach. Her clothes were simple, and her sandals were dirty, but you could also tell she was someone who was a beautiful spirit and held an internal strength.

I thought, *To be out there on your own with three kids in a type of environment that's dangerous for women and children, you had to have some type of smarts about you.*

After the case workers did their part, I proceeded to ask her about her children, which the translator conveyed to her. She shared with me that her children were 14, 6, and 4-years-old. I noticed she was fairly coherent, and had no problem answering questions. She also didn't interrupt, and her mannerisms were very respectful. She didn't seem mentally ill, and if I hadn't known about the back history, I would never have placed that label on her. Then again, I'm not a doctor.

Suddenly, I saw a flashlight beaming from the cracks of the house—one of her kids probably.

"What are your children doing now?"

"My kids are studying," she said.

I raised my eyebrows.

"Yes, they go to school."

I turned to ask the workers, "From what I understand, the only way they can go to school is if they have an address, correct?"

It's important to note in Chile it was illegal for anyone to build a shelter or structure on private or government property. It would be torn down within days. Also, I knew that in order for children to get free public education, they must have a physical address. Otherwise, they would be considered nonresidents and would not have access to any education whatsoever. So, my question stemmed from these two facts.

"Her kids *do* go to school," the translator said.

I told the translator, "Please ask her how it's possible for her to maintain a place to live in, and second, how has she managed to have all three of her children in school? Every day, hundreds of families living on the streets are continually on the move because they have no place to sleep, no address, and none of their children go to school."

I said, "Ask her, are they going to a school we don't know about?"

As she began to answer, she spoke a bit differently and carried herself in a unique way. *It's probably why they thought she was mentally ill,* I thought. However, in order to be an agent of change in this situation, I knew I had to see far beyond what others typically saw and thought of her - and the

1% I spoke of earlier. **As she continued to answer, I noticed that she was now becoming extremely shy.** Her head then fell forward while momentarily glancing upward to see if anyone were really listening. My heart went out to her. It appeared she was feeling a bit uncomfortable about what she was explaining. However, I knew it was important to be patient. When she finished, the translator made a slight sign, paused for a minute, looked at her and then turned toward me. What followed next was the most amazing thing I'd ever heard there.

He said, "Erik, she said she's been here for almost four years. During this time, she found some people to help her make this small shelter. How she is able to live here is interesting as well."

He pointed up to the freeway above our heads and said, "She told me that under this overpass is the border in between two municipalities. Therefore, this small piece of land is sort of no-man's-land. Technically, it's not even on the map. So, she made her home here."

"María works at night collecting cardboard while her children sleep. She's saving up to hopefully someday to get enough money for a down payment on a government-subsidized home."

My heart filled with amazement. I couldn't believe what I was hearing. *She's been out here in this spot for four years?*

I said anxiously, "What about the education? Her kids can't go to school unless they have an address."

He smiled. "Ah yes, sorry I didn't tell you that part. Since she's wedged in between two legal streets, but apparently the place she built her home on isn't really registered with the city, she made up her own street name and address and wrote down the two real ones as the nearest intersection on the forms. That way, her children would have an address and could go to school. Kind of funny, actually."

"Funny?" *More like genius!* I thought. My heart was bursting for her.

I stopped and looked at her eyes for a moment, and then I asked the translator to translate as I spoke from my heart to hers. I said, "María, I spent the last couple of months traveling all through Peru and here in Chile, meeting several mothers and children in similar situations, living on the streets, abandoned, but I've never met someone as intelligent and resourceful as you have been."

I crouched down just so I could look up at her as she tilted her head to the ground.

I told the translator and the caseworkers very seriously to translate exactly what I said next, ensuring that it was loud enough so her children could hear my words being translated.

My support team stared at me a bit shocked. I didn't care what they thought.

I continued, "Not only do you have the intelligence, creativity, and determination to build a home for you and your children, you have done it in a way that thousands of other homeless families have not, and to add to that, you found a way for your children to go to school."

"You, in my eyes, and I'm sure in God's eyes, are much more than what others have labeled you— you are a gifted and outstanding person, mother, and woman. **You aren't disabled or mentally challenged and those who fail to see the greatness in you really need to take a deeper look—not at you, but at themselves."**

She started to cry. I rose up from my knees and just had to hug her; I didn't care if it was appropriate or not. It was from my heart, and I was immensely inspired by what she had told me.

She wiped the tears from her eyes, you could tell nobody had spoken to her like this before. I said, "Can I meet your children?"

Her face lit up, "Yes, they're over there."

As we walked past her fire ablaze in the old rusty canister, her kids ran out of the small shelter.

"What's this?" I said smiling. "How could three kids and a mother fit inside there?"

The shelter was even smaller than I had thought, no bigger than a guest bathroom in a standard house! As they got closer, they all apologized for coming out so late but explained it was because they were just finishing their homework for class in the morning.

I asked the boy to tell me about school. Did he like it?

"I really enjoy it," he said. "But all my friends think I live in a house. None of them know I live here."

He looked down in embarrassment.

"I understand," I said.

I told him when I was a child there was a time when I lived in a park and I couldn't go to school because we had no car. I told him, "These things are temporary as long as you choose to be good and do good things and not try to take a short cut."

Then he told me he wanted to be an airplane mechanic. My mouth dropped open. *Who thinks of that?*

I knew that the *Hogar* staff was testing the children for general math and reading aptitude. So, I decided to tell him a story. I said to him, "When I was in school, they tested us one time to find out if we would be a leader or a follower, and what do you think the result was? I came out with a glowing assessment of being a follower, never a leader! My teacher said it out loud to the whole class," I added.

He smiled.

"My guidance counselor even told me I would be a florist when I grew up. But I didn't end up being a florist; instead I ended up building a few companies, and more importantly, meeting some great and gifted people around the world – like you."

What I desperately wanted to get across to him was that even the experts don't know what we are destined for. How could they know? They only see the 1%. I wanted to tell him, don't let other people's labels determine your story. A homeless kid—*that's a label.*

I pointed at the little shelter behind him and said, "These challenges you have now are a gift and preparation for other things you need to do moving forward. Sometimes our lives are either a warning or an inspiration; and you have a choice to make your life an inspiration."

I don't remember the rest of the conversation. I do remember how much strength that young boy had, and I really wished I could have stayed in touch with him. In my mind, he was just as inspirational as his mother.

He reminded me of a speaker I saw once in Toronto who helped people labeled with mental disabilities get into the workforce. His story was very memorable. He was talking about how he was an American with a company of over 200 employees, but he had once been a foster child who hadn't learn how to read or write until he was an adult because he was diagnosed with dyslexia and held back in school. He had so many things against him, yet he focused on what he knew and built a successful construction business.

He used this analogy to describe his success: if God gives you a one-string guitar and everyone else has six strings, you play that one string so loudly and so strongly, that it surpasses everyone else around you.

In my opinion, María was an excellent one-stringed guitar player. Hopefully, her son would be, too.

Later, I laid down on the back seat of the van with my eyes open listening to the *Hogar* caseworkers chatting before we left the site. From time to time the translator would translate their words for me. I understood they were talking about how dangerous it was being homeless in Chile, people going missing off the streets, being potentially taken for their kidneys, rumors of supposed organ snatching. **They were also talking about separating children from their homeless parents, and that, in many cases, it was necessary.** I disagreed; I didn't think that was always the best solution. Certainly, it wasn't in María's case.

Sometimes, the power of what a mother has inside of her, not what she doesn't have on the outside, can be very inspirational for a child. I closed my eyes and silently, I thanked María for her gift to us and her family, and for her permission to share her inspirational and powerful story with others.

The Shantytown Souls

***

As we drove up, two armed guards pulled open the metal gates, and let us through.

My last few days in Chile, I had arranged a visit to the slums. Even though Chile is one of the most prosperous country in Latin America, in 2006, the poverty rate was about 29% and now is about 8%. However, inequality is still too high. The richest 20% earn 10 times more than the poorest 20% in 2006. In 2017, the inequality had fallen to 8.9 times.

That day I was with a small grassroots organization that worked with a handful of children in a community way below the poverty line. I felt very honored, as I knew I was one of the few foreigners who would ever get the luxury of going inside this self-policed "gated" community. As we drove through, I saw rows and rows of shanty houses and people walking along makeshift alleys.

I was entering a completely different world.

The first thing I noticed was that there wasn't a bit of green inside: no grass anywhere, no parks or trees. Everything was dry, dirty, and made out of either mud, rocks, or discarded building materials. As we drove slowly through the town, it looked like houses that rose up out of an emptied garbage dump. It was very dusty, and by the smell that would come and go, I could tell there was no sewer system, but it wasn't bad enough to roll up the window.

It reminded me of what I'd seen from photos of the *favelas* (shantytowns) in Brazil. **I would never have expected to find something like this in a city as developed as Santiago.** Even more amazing was that it was just a mile or two from a Home Depot. The existence of this small shantytown juxtaposed with the reality of the industrialized and commercialized city all around it was nauseating.

I noticed the power lines overhead had masses of wires coming in and out of the meters, which had obviously been tampered with. They'd built their own power grid and were syphoning electricity from nearby. I reached for my camera but one of the volunteers motioned for me to stop.

"No photos allowed," she said.

Three volunteers were in the car with me that day. Their job was to be a sort of conduit for the people inside of this community and the outside world, bringing them basic necessities, like medical supplies, clothing, food, and child services. As we approached the daycare, I reminded myself that I was there to learn as much as I could about their programs and spend time with the children. No matter how bad it was, I wanted to see and understand, first hand, what condition they were in and how the children thrived (or otherwise) in such a place.

In the middle of the community was a small area surrounded by a cheaply made wire fence, no bigger than 500 square feet. One of the volunteers informed me the fencing was put around it to keep out the drug dealers and prostitutes. It looked flimsy. The fence was tight enough to prevent you putting your hand through it, but you could probably run it down on a bicycle. I didn't feel I was in any danger in this area, but maybe that was because the only thing I could see were the kids.

Inside the fencing, playing on a little patch of dirt, were about half a dozen children. Some of them were digging in the sandbox, others were running around playing, being kids. The space was rudimentary, something you'd expect to see a dog chained up in, not a playground, but if you looked hard enough, you could see the miracles, as if little seedlings were coming up out of the dry cracked earth, oblivious to what was around them. It was like a magical garden to me.

Inside the enclosure, I was immediately swarmed by small warm bodies and curious faces. The children were all talking to me at once in Spanish, of course, as if I could understand them. I just stared at their faces in awe with a big smile; they were the most beautiful children I'd ever seen. Each was so unique. **I know it sounds strange to say, but it was almost like meeting all my friends from the past all at once.**

They weren't in the best of shape, to be honest. Not one of them was entirely clean; dirt mixed with snot covered their noses, and some were a lot dirtier than others. But I felt their desire to be noticed and for someone to be present with them. They wanted my attention. I felt bad I couldn't speak with them, so I spoke in English. They didn't care or seem to get frustrated; we were having fun.

After that, we went inside for crafts. I didn't know what to say, so I improvised. I sat across from one of the little girls and we had a funny face contest, which was awesome. (Funny faces are a universal language.)

Maybe because there was no institution around us, no formal schedule, no charts hanging on the walls, the interactions were more intense. I could relax and get to know the children better. I was blown away at how well-mannered some of these kids were. Even compared with the children I had seen at *Hogar*, there was a distinct absence of depression or anxiety in them. They weren't awkward or aggressive, nobody was curled up in the corner crying. Despite needing some proper shoes and a good lice comb, they were just very well-rounded healthy children. I found it fascinating.

I thought that if they were dressed in clean clothes and put in a private school, their attitudes wouldn't have been any different.

A few of them hugged me. I had to be very mindful because I didn't know what was appropriate or not. Even if you wanted so badly to scoop them up and hug them, you had to respect space and protocols.

I enjoyed it so much, I arranged to come back the next day and work with the children. I also wanted to try to learn a bit more about their programs and how they were funded. Over the next few days, I asked the volunteers a lot of questions. **My biggest question was how did they raise money?**

Because it was a shantytown, the staff told me they were largely dependent on government subsidies. In fact, I had come at the end of the three-year project where they had been documenting all the people in the town—their names, how many people were in each family, how many kids, and so on—and they had just delivered this report to the government of Chile in hopes of getting approved for more funding. Things were looking hopeful.

I was so happy for them. Not only did I get to find these little "seeds" growing in this garden, I knew their lives would change for the better soon. There was definitely a note of concern in the volunteers' voices; you could tell they wanted the best for these children. The longer they were prevented from going to school and socializing with other kids, the worse it would be for them.

It was hard for me to wrap my head around how completely isolated these kids were. The staff told me one time they'd raised enough money to hire a bus and take the children to a local park, but when the bus pulled up, the kids wouldn't get inside the bus because they'd never been inside something that moves. Then, when they arrived at the park, the kids all stood up on their seats and started yelling, **"Look at the funny mountains!" (They'd never seen buildings before.)**

I couldn't imagine it. *At six years old, and they didn't know what a building was.* That's how isolated they were. I hoped that once they got the government funding, the kids would be able to take regular field trips, and maybe even attend one of the local schools.

The last day, I went to the shantytown and the staff took me into the building. I began playing with the children as usual. A few minutes later the volunteers ran into the room; they looked panicked.

"We have to leave right now," they said.

I was sitting talking to the little girl, the one with the funny faces and pigtails.

"What's wrong?"

"The government is forcing their way in with their trucks."

We left immediately. When they tell you it's time to go, you have to go.

Later in the car, the staff told me what had happened. The plot the shantytown was on was premium land in the heart of the city, near Home Depot. It was too valuable, and too close to a developing area. The government had gotten all the information they needed from them, and they had no intention of funding the shantytown, just cleaning it out. They only wanted to know how many people were there so they could fill the trucks and get them all out.

I felt disgusted. It appeared they'd been completely betrayed.

What about the children? I wondered. I asked, "Where are they going to go?"

Nobody knew.

I was just a day away from leaving for Argentina; I felt totally helpless. The staff dropped me off at the hostel, I gave them Diana's email address and asked them to stay in touch. They were in tears.

Unfortunately, I had to fly out the next day for Argentina. As I watched Santiago's green landscape fade beneath the clouds on the plane, I reflected sadly on the events that had happened the day before. I couldn't possibly imagine that my trip would get any more intense than it was in Chile. **In the Chilean people I had seen undeniable proof of human ingenuity, resourcefulness, and love overcoming the worst of circumstances, but external forces couldn't always be predicted.** At any moment, life can change.

Unfortunately, I didn't even have a chance to say goodbye to the kids.

Today, when I look at the pictures of these children, I could stare at them for moments without end. I don't know why, but I still have a lot of hopes for them. Did they go to an orphanage? Or were they dispersed around the city, and put into urban housing? Scattered like seeds on the wind. I wish I could have watched them grow up from afar. It would be a dream for me. It's one thing to help a child, but another thing to watch over them to make sure they're safe. **Whenever I think of them, all I can remember is how we played and laughed together.**

Part Two

Argentina:
The Devil Wants
to Tango

May 2006
Buenos Aires, Argentina

***

I flew into Buenos Aires airport, the capitol of Argentina. When I landed, I went directly to the hostel on 208 Maipu, just steps away from the Metropolitan Cathedral and the Obelisco de Buenos Aires. I had a few days before I started volunteering and I wanted to capture some moments through the lens of my camera.

If I had to describe Argentina back then, I would say the city was "Old World" with a lot of character. The core of Buenos Aires was filled with neoclassical buildings and architecture with French and Italian influences. I strolled along the wide boulevards with hundreds of other tourists and stood in the plazas to take photos of monumental statues and fountains that had withstood the test of time. People told me that Argentina was similar to Europe, and I could see why.

Buenos Aires was the most historically rich city I'd visited in my journey so far. I later learned that the rest of Latin America would describe Argentinians as proud and even arrogant, but I didn't see it that day. Maybe because I wasn't told this to label them beforehand.

It was also the first city where I really started taking a lot more pictures of people in general, and specifically the expressions on their faces. That day, I was obsessed with capturing people in those candid moments when they were being uniquely themselves. **From a homeless man's smile to the intense concentration of a street artist drawing someone's portrait,** I didn't want to forget any of the joy, tenderness, or moments of genuine happiness I saw there.

Later in the afternoon, I found myself in an outdoor shopping center on the promenade taking photos of the different artists on the street. I didn't care so much about what they were wearing or doing, just the tension (or lack of it) in their faces as a direct reflection of what was in their eyes. There was no shortage of tango dancers, mimes, human statues, or countless other people expressing themselves for me to focus on, but one scene in particular stood out.

In the middle of a busy city center, I saw a family—a father, mother, and four children, ages one through five—sitting on a blanket on the sidewalk. They weren't openly begging with desperate faces or hands out, but you could tell by the bags of belongings on the ground beside them, they were probably homeless. The father was sitting cross-legged on the ground with a guitar on his knee, smiling proudly and singing while strumming. Respectfully, I stopped to listen to him play.

Something about this scene struck me: they had dignity. If you had taken the same family and put them on a stage, the feeling would have been no different. **The image of that father captivated the moment.** As much as it moved me seeing an entire family on the streets of Buenos Aires asking for money, all I could do was honor and respect them. Not only the bravery of the parents for being there, but their courage to even get up in the morning in the face of what most of us would describe as hardships and do it with a smile.

I thought, *To have that type of strength to sit there with your children with your head held high is something extraordinary.*

Standing there, totally engrossed in the expression on the father's face while he played guitar, I realized I'd seen that look of pride and faith somewhere before. My memory taking me back, I realized it was my father.

We were separated from my father when I was 7 years old, and I didn't reunite with him in any meaningful way until I was 19 (basically a grown man), so my memories of him are scarce. Still, his values and the memories of him left a strong impression on me as a child.

My father was a Buddhist and he didn't talk much, but he wasn't silent either. He was tall (almost as tall as me), quite slender, and always wore suits. An executive chef by trade, he was proud of two things: his Japanese heritage (he insisted all the best things came from Japan), and his kitchen, which he ran with meticulous precision. He had two simple rules in his kitchen: no swearing (respect among the staff was number one), and no radio (you were there to work).

He used to take me to his walk-in fridge and show me how clean it was inside. He'd pull the boxes up and show me the floor underneath. "Why are you showing me the floor, dad," I asked?

"It's spotless," he said.

I remember visiting him at work and seeing the employees looking at my father with respect; it made me even more proud of him.

My father was dignified, yet he wasn't arrogant at all. As an executive chef, he had cooked for a King, a Prince, and several global leaders and actors in his time. However, in his eyes, the most important person in his kitchen was his Dishwasher. He would say, "Without clean dishes none of us could do our jobs; we couldn't serve our customers." Even though he had cooked delicacies for celebrities and dignitaries all over the world, his favorite go-to food after work was a greasy burger, or some Chinese noodles. He wasn't afraid to dig in and enjoy the simplest of foods.

Growing up without my father or a reliable environment created a lot of hurt and anger in me, and, as a result, I pushed my father away for a long time. By the time I was 26 years old, he had moved back to Canada, and after all that time, he would call me and say, "Erik, I want to see you."

At the same time, my business was taking off, so it provided me with an easy excuse to avoid seeing him. I'd say, "Sorry, I can't this weekend," whenever he called. But what I really felt like telling him was, "You weren't there for all these years and now you want to see me?" **Part of me wanted to punish him for not being there, another part of me didn't want to get close and open the wound again, and another part of me just didn't want to make the time, as I had so many other priorities at the time.**

It went on like this until, one day, I had an insight at a Tony Robbins event.

Back then, I was a volunteer mic runner. Tony would point to someone in the crowd and I would go dashing through rows of people to hand the mic to them. That day, Tony pointed at a woman and I ran over with the mic as I had done countless times. Little did I know I was about to encounter something that would shake my beliefs to the core. I remember her story was quite sad; she said her husband and her were basically roommates, and they were just staying together for the kids.

At that moment, Tony interrupted her and yelled, "Bullshit!"

The woman stopped talking and dropped the mic to her side, looking sad and quite shocked.

"If you want to show your kids that a loving marriage is about two people living in separate rooms and sleeping in separate beds, then you're doing them more harm than good," he said.

I felt like he'd thrown a brick at me; it was the words "more harm than good." I remember crouching at her feet, holding the mic over my head, frozen, and I had this perplexing thought, *Wait a minute... If my father had been part of my life growing up... if they didn't separate, who would I be today?*

I am who I am today *because* my father and mother separated, not the other way around. My father wasn't a violent man, but when he was married to my mother, it brought out the worst in both of them. They argued often and fought bitterly. My mother always spoke her mind, and she was insecure and needy too in that relationship. On the other hand, my father was strict and orderly. So, you had these two opposing forces, my mother who craved attention and love, and my father, who wanted respect first. It would have been a disaster if they'd tried to stay together.

Like the Oprah Winfrey quote, "Turn your wounds into wisdom," I had a transformational moment, and was ready to forgive my father.

The second I got home I called my dad right away, and said, "I want you to come spend the weekend at my house."

He politely accepted my invitation, but I could tell he was shocked.

The next weekend, my father came to see me at my house in Caledon. He cooked for me in my own kitchen, which was delightful. After lunch we were having a quiet moment at the kitchen table, and suddenly, he got up and started doing dishes. I remember sitting there watching in awe as my father filled the sink with soapy water, rinsed each dish, fork, and knife, and carefully dried them. It was like watching a natural wonder, or a live birth, and I was surprisingly dumbfounded.

I said, "Dad, I didn't know you washed dishes."

"I always wash dishes," he said, drying his hands on the dish towel. "A chef should be able to take care of a meal from beginning to end. All the work in my kitchen is of equal importance."

It was such a simple moment, but it spoke volumes to me about my dad's humility, values, and work ethic.

Unsure of what to do with my father for the rest of the day, I decided to take him to a *Harry Rosen*, a high-end clothing and suit store in Toronto where they sell designer clothes like Versace, Armani, and Gucci, among others. My father was always well dressed. Every day he'd go into work in a suit and change into his chef's clothes. I thought the least I could do was take him shopping for a new one.

Before we went inside *Harry Rosen,* I stopped him in the entryway of the brightly lit department store. He looked at me with confusion. I told him, "Dad do you remember when I was a young boy and you took me to *Consumers Distributing* on my birthday and you said, 'you can have anything you want for your birthday?'"

He nodded. "Yes."

"Now it's my turn," I said, gesturing at the racks of dress shirts, jackets, and pants. "Any suit you want in the store you can have—any suit you like."

My father sort of drew himself up and tightened his lips into a frown. "No," he said, shaking his head. He paused as if searching for what to say next and replied after what felt like minutes later,

"I only buy Japanese suits."

Wow, I thought. I had put my heart (and wallet) on the table; I tried to give him a gift, but he turned it down. I'd never heard of any Japanese suit designers personally (and frankly, I found it a little arrogant). But I thought, *Okay, his decision.*

He insisted I buy something for myself that day instead, which I did, and then we left the store.

The next morning it was like nothing had happened. He was up early, making scrambled eggs and talking about how beautiful it was to hear the birds singing in the yard in the morning (I'd never noticed the birds before), and I was surprised how connected my father was to nature. That was our weekend. A year later, he called me into his office and told me he had liver cancer. I broke into tears. **Three years later, he died.** He was 57 years old.

At the funeral, all I could think was, *What if I hadn't forgiven my father? What if I'd held onto the false beliefs that kept us apart?* We wouldn't have had those three years together. My heart was completely filled and healed by this, but I had an even bigger shock coming. That day at the funeral, just before we gathered in the room to pay our last respects, one of my father's closest friends came up to me and said, "I have to tell you something about your dad."

He proceeded to tell me one night my father called him up and he was crying. "Your dad does not cry—and he was *really* crying," he said. "So, I asked him desperately, 'what's wrong?'"

My father told him, between catching his breath, "Guess what my son did for me today? He took me to a store and told me anything I wanted I could have."

When he told me this, I felt like someone stuck a nine-inch nail into my heart. I had pushed my father aside that day in the *Harry Rosen*, not truly understanding what he was feeling. I didn't realize he cared so deeply in that moment, and that it hurt him to show it to me.

How easily we misunderstand the actions of others, and why they do the things they do, especially our parents…

We cannot truly know what someone is going through, or the hurt they bury inside. We never know the whole story. That look of pride, or shame, or joy, or anger in someone's eyes, all we see is what they allow us to see, and what we believe about them is only a small percentage of who they really are and what they're feeling.

The sun was setting, and my feet were sore from walking miles around the city. It was time to get back to the hostel. My first day in Buenos Aires had been enlightening, to say the least.

As I stood in the promenade, watching this Argentinian father playing beautiful music to feed his family, I wondered if that look of heartfelt pride was to hide his true feelings. I looked at his young children by his side, and I wondered if his sons and daughters would grow up knowing how much he loved them.

Hostel Living

✳✳✳

By this time, I had some experience with hostels, and I knew what I was getting into. Still, the place I stayed at in Buenos Aires would be an even more elevating and atypical experience.

The building was tall and extremely narrow. Inside, I walked up the short flight of stairs that led to a small reception desk, which I passed on the way up. The staff greeted me briefly, but they weren't overly friendly. The main floor opened up into a separate living room with oversized windows that faced and framed the classical facade of the building across the street. There were a couple of Ikea style couches where guests could socialize and chill out. The decor was minimal: white colonial style plaster walls and wood accents. Nothing fancy, but the hostel was generally clean and comfortable.

I headed up to the second floor where I would be staying. I had already booked my room online, which I knew was a co-ed sleeping quarters shared with nine other people. **Before my trip to South America, I hadn't exercised my social skills much; I was comfortable being in my own zone.** I hoped that sharing a room with other travelers would force me to grow and enjoy socializing and meeting other amazing people.

The room was extremely basic. I felt a little nervous when I saw the bunk beds because they were crudely constructed, it looked like they were made out of 2 x 4's. Nobody else seemed concerned, but I opted for the top bunk anyway, as it felt slightly safer.

The first person I met in the room was a young woman named Marianne from New York. I came to learn she had grown up in foster care and had been adopted, and with a few shared stories, we bonded without hesitation. Then I met a couple from the UK, and an Irish gentleman. There were also some rambunctious ladies from New York City who had a peculiar habit of washing their undergarments in the bathroom and hanging them all over the room to dry— even on my bed! It was a unique mix of people, I felt if you tried to put every type of person into one room, this is what it would look like.

The dynamics in that room became even more interesting over the next few days as we attempted to live with each other in such close quarters. I have to admit, I was tempted to stay at a hotel a few times.

The first night, we learned the young man from Ireland liked to exorbitantly enjoy his alcohol. One night in particular, he stumbled into the room in the wee hours, crashing into things and reeking of alcohol. The next night, he did the same thing. Nobody said anything to him about it in the morning, we just let him sleep it off. **A few nights later, we were awakened at 3am by strange noises in the room, it sounded like water.** Someone switched on the light, and we all screamed— he was weaving from side to side, pants down, peeing on someone's backpack.

"I thought this was the washroom," he mumbled.

The entire room came together that night and insisted the hostel do something. **Finally, they called the police, and he was officially banned from the hostel.**

Great, I thought. Now we could all get a good night's sleep without fear of being woken up. Unfortunately, we had another problem.

The next night, after midnight, I awoke to the bed lightly shaking. Maríanne was in the top bunk across from mine, staring at me with wide eyes. Silently, she pointed to the guy in the bunk down below me. I looked down, squinting in the darkness trying to make out what was happening. It appeared he was moving his hands under the covers. I thought, *What is he doing down there?* Then I realized what he was doing.

Embarrassed, I laid back down and squeezed my eyes shut, and prayed I would fall asleep quick. Fortunately, he only stayed a couple of nights. (Thank God.)

If my nighttime experiences were interesting, my daytime adventures would be no less jarring. Argentina was a completely different culture, and I made a lot of little faux pas. For instance, in Argentina they eat at a much later time than what I was used to. Every time I went out looking for some dinner everything was closed! Finally, I figured out the proper time to eat dinner in Buenos Aires, but I still had the problem of the language barrier. One time, I was in a French restaurant enjoying a meal by myself and I waved the waiter over to ask him for some butter. This was one of those fancy places where the staff dressed in black with little white aprons and carried silver trays in their hands. I tried to say it in Spanish, but he gave me an odd look.

I repeated the statement, "poquito besito?" (I thought I was saying "a little butter")

Again, he gave me a really strange look, almost like he was offended. I wasn't sure what I had done wrong. Finally, he walked away in disgust. Later, I looked up the word *besito* in the Spanish dictionary—he thought I was asking for a little *kiss*! To this day, the thought of it makes me laugh out loud. His reaction was priceless.

In these unfamiliar surroundings, going through all these strange and confusing experiences, I started to really miss Diana. It felt like she was the only thing familiar to me, and I kept reaching out to her for support. During the first few days, we tried to video chat over Skype, but there wasn't always a reliable Internet connection, so we wrote long emails to each other instead. Every morning I would wake up excited to check my inbox to see if Diana had written me back. At night, I would lay in my top bunk bed for hours and listen to Jack Johnson, and Bryan Adams. I would sing the lyrics of *All for Love* and think, *It's about us!*

Long distance relationships can be like that, you build a future fantasy about the relationship, and it leads you deeper and deeper into an illusion of love. By this time, I was happily filled and spirited by it all, and quite immersed in it.

The Nuns Home for Children
✳✳✳

I looked across the blacktop at the blur of bodies in motion in front of me. Just left of center field, one of the boys got possession and was rapidly headed in my direction. With a look of fierce concentration on his face he maneuvered the ball down the field. I lowered my stance and opened my arms out wide in anticipation of the kick.

I dove— but the ball sailed over my fingertips and right in between the metal posts.

I heard the kids scream, "Goooal!"

My teammates groaned.

When the kids asked me to play soccer with them that day, I said yes, thinking it would be fun. I just wished I could have lived up to their expectations that day. The first problem was they were playing on the concrete, not grass, and the second problem was that they were using a basketball, not a soccer ball, and it hurt like hell. **Every time I got smacked with it, I had to remind myself I was a grown man,** and these were children, 10 to 14 years old. I couldn't back down.

As the game progressed, and the kids witnessed my lack of soccer playing skills, they gradually demoted me. First, they made me a forward, then goalie, and finally after this last goal, one of the players politely motioned for me to sit the next round out.

Fine by me, I thought with a smile. I was tired of getting hit with that basketball.

Limping over to the picnic benches on the sidelines, I sat down to watch the rest of the game. My thighs were sore, I was sure I was going to find bruises and bumps all up and down my legs later. I had to laugh. For the first time in my life (not even when I was 11) I got benched by 12-year-olds!

I had lined up two organizations to volunteer at before arriving in Argentina. This was the first, and, by far, the largest orphanage I had seen on my mission across South America. The complex took up an entire city block and was composed of several large buildings with metal gates in front, surrounded by a massive concrete wall. **As intimidating as it appeared on the outside, inside was bustling with life.** Once you entered the compound, a large courtyard led to the front steps of the school. Behind this were the children's rooms and the playground where we played soccer that day.

My first few days, the staff gave me a tour of the facilities and told me more about their programs, housing, and medical support for the children, which included psychologists who were available to the children to support them in their mental health and development. I didn't find anything overly unique or outstanding about their programs through my research at this time; they all seemed pretty standard. However, I was surprised at how few people could care for so many children.

The foundation was home to over three hundred children who lived and went to school there, along with dozens more children who came during the daytime and left at night. Twelve nuns ran the facility along with a small staff of volunteers. **For the most part, they made do with what they had, whether that was limited staff, food, or supplies.**

As I walked around, I noticed some areas were a little run down. I saw peeling paint on the walls, metal bars on the windows of the children's bedrooms, and wires hanging out of the concrete walls. It reminded me less of a school and more of an industrial building where there might have been a fabrication process, but still there were a few familiar childhood amenities like swing sets, a soccer "field," and a recreation room with a small 25" television to watch movies and some bus seats that had been recycled into lounge chairs. Everywhere I went, I saw the children cleaning and taking care of the building. They put aprons on and washed vegetables in the kitchen or swept dirt in the hallways.

After the soccer game, we went inside to have some lunch with the children. The nuns handed me a large plate and I looked down at the sausage and pile of beans with mixed feelings. I was starving and it smelled delicious, but I felt conflicted about how much food I'd been served— it was much more than everyone else. I don't think I've ever felt guilty while eating before, so this was new to me. I stood there for a few seconds, debating on whether I should give it back. I decided if I didn't eat the food it would be even more disrespectful. So, I did eat it, but very slowly and mindfully.

That day, I worked with the children in their classes, and afterward, I sat with them while they did their math or English homework. I discovered the children were from all over Argentina, and I was also surprised and a bit dismayed to see a lot of siblings in this place. I learned that, sometimes, mothers would have more than one child and drop them off at the center to join their brothers and sisters.

I thought, *what about the mothers? What about the fathers?* There were no programs, no help for these parents. I understood there wasn't much that the nuns could do, they obviously had their hands full. **But I wondered how many of these mothers were just children themselves and needed counseling and services.** I was trying to figure out some way to do something, so I started searching for a program that might address the problem.

"Be careful," Diana said when I spoke with her about it on the phone. "If you say you want to help the mothers, they might see you in the wrong way."

Taking her comments into consideration, I decided she was right, and my time was limited to the task at hand. I needed to stay focused on my core mission, so I put this project aside and went back to concentrating on the children. Unfortunately, the nuns were very strict (I wouldn't have expected otherwise), and under the watchful eye of these ladies in dark blue robes and starched white habits, I wasn't able to spend as much time with the children as I had in other organizations. So, I invested the remainder of my days observing and noting the processes of the nuns, all while admiring their discipline and care for the children. Honestly, it was the single most systematic thing I'd seen.

Every day, the sisters took the children through their daily routine of prayer, breakfast, lessons, lunch, more lessons, soccer, and evening prayer before a very early bedtime. Considering they did all this with limited resources and no business management background, just hard work and faith, I was thoroughly impressed and intrigued.

After studying their system for days, I decided to do something nice for both the nuns and the children, a small gesture of appreciation. Before going to work at the orphanage, I went down to a local store and bought twelve brand new soccer balls. At that time, the World Cup was playing, so I knew the children would really appreciate this.

That morning I strolled in, proudly holding a huge bag of official soccer balls in my hands. I was thinking, *maybe this will get me a promotion!* As soon as the nun saw me, she pointed at me and said, "Come."

Seeing her chilly demeanor wiped the smile off my face.

She didn't look at me, she just walked me diligently, but without hurrying, to her office. Inside, she shut the door and sat me in the chair opposite from her. I wondered, *did I do something wrong?* I looked at her with a concerned, yet childish grin. **I was having flashbacks of being sent to the principal's office when I was in high school.**

She pointed at the soccer balls and said in a restrained tone, "Leave these here. You aren't allowed to give gifts to the kids."

I trusted she was doing this for a very good reason, and this was her house, not mine. But I had to admit, I was a little shocked and upset. I never understood if she intended to give the soccer balls to the children or not, but I accepted the fact that I should have asked permission beforehand.

After the sting from this "slap on the wrist" had subsided, and gradually as the weeks went by, I found myself less intimidated by these nuns, and even more in awe of them. When I sat back watching their work, I realized I was always content being with them. They would speak slowly to me in Spanish and broken English, while I tried my best to understand. I wasn't overthinking it, just listening and being present with them. Gradually, I began to see the nuns as steadfast and altruistic gifts to these children, as people like you and me, who get tired, frustrated, and sometimes don't have all the answers. They did what was necessary.

Adjacent to the school was a garden where the nuns tended to their vegetables, fruits, and flowers. On my last day of volunteering, I asked them if it was okay to take a few pictures of them working in the garden. I wanted to remember these caretakers, not just working with the children, but around other beautiful elements of the facility. They granted me permission, so I began to take pictures of them as they trimmed and watered the flowering trees and fragrant bushes, with families of geese, ducks, and chickens at their feet, roaming free around the yard. The nuns tolerated me with an amused patience and occasionally even smiled for the camera.

Sitting in this beautiful growing garden with these patient gardeners, I had a realization. I thought, *We can still connect without saying anything.* We were just using wordless communication. You can speak without words, hear without judging, feel without thought, and touch without giving. Sometimes, the best way to touch someone's heart is to just be present with them in that moment and help them see the gifts and the beauty that's already inside of them instead of trying to fix them or change them.

The Devil Wants to Tango

***

"Lord make me an instrument of your peace; where there is hatred, let me sow love; where there is injury, pardon; where there is discord, union; where there is doubt, faith; where there is despair, hope; where there is darkness, light; and where there is sadness, joy."

—St. Francis of Assisi

One of the things I noticed about Argentina was that the devil liked to dance at night.

I don't know if this was typical of Buenos Aires, but I would often see strip clubs, with prostitutes and strippers standing in the dark alleys, off the beaten path of main tourist areas. I had to walk by these "establishments" so often as I approached the hostel, it got to the point where people began to come up to me on the street. To my shock, some of them were even brazen enough to touch my arm. I was a young, unmarried man back then, and I understood that I was a target, but it made me wonder, *Am I giving off a desperate vibe?*

One evening, I was walking back from the orphanage, absorbed in my thoughts and not focusing the environment around me. I was exhausted from being with the children all day, I was missing Diana terribly, and I was still a bit bummed about the soccer ball thing. Out of the corner of my eye, I noticed a man detach himself from the shadows and slide up behind me on the street. I glanced quickly over my shoulder to find him following me at a close distance.

Not again, I thought.

I was doing my usual thing, ignoring him and hoping he'd go away, but he didn't seem to be taking the hint. I could hear his footsteps steadily getting louder on the pavement right behind me. **My senses were on alert, my shoulders were tense, teeth clenched, and heart pounding.** Being nice clearly wasn't working, and I'd had enough. Finally, I turned around and yelled at him, "Get the fuck away from me!"

My whole body was vibrating, I was so angry.

He took a couple of steps back with a startled look on his face, as if my words had physically hurt him.

It was so unlike me, I even shocked myself.

Spending every day with these children, worrying about their futures, and being so open and vulnerable for such a long period of time, had stretched my heart wide open. I was beginning to wonder how far I could go seeing so much pain and desperation, before I would snap. It was a little scary. That night, as I passed by the same people beckoning me into their strip club or sex show, seeing all these temptations, the clubs, the women, I realized it was starting to pick away at me.

When I arrived at the hostel, I immediately went to the computer center to check my email. I needed something to take me out of the darkness and away from provoking thoughts that crowded my brain. I thought, at the very least, maybe Diana had written me. In my inbox there was an email from one of the potential clients in California I had been negotiating a seven-figure contract with, and I clicked on it eagerly. I had been diligently working on my plans for my next company, and this money would allow me to continue volunteering for a long time, and maybe even start a charitable program of my own.

As I read the first two sentences of the email, my stomach dropped. I sat there frozen, my shoulders fell, and my hands went numb. I looked down at my dirty sneakers in disbelief. They were letting me know they were rescinding the offer; I had lost the contract.

In one day, my entire future plans for continuing this work and even building a foundation in South America were shut down.

The reality of the situation, along with my fears and my concerns for the future came forward and engulfed me like a tidal wave. I don't drink to escape; so, like other normal people do, I went for some ice cream.

It was late at night, around 11pm, when I left the hostel. I decided to play it safe and go to a busy area to see what I could find. In the promenade I saw a makeshift ice cream shop, with just a few small round tables and some aluminum chairs out front. *Good enough,* I thought.

At the counter, I ordered a vanilla soft serve in a cone, and went outside to sit and enjoy it. While I was ordering, I had seen some little girls out of the corner of my eye, standing in front of the shop. This was the first time I'd seen young girls by themselves on the street at night. When I walked outside, I got a better look at them. At a glance I could tell they were homeless. They were maybe 4 and 6 years old, with long matted brown hair, torn shirts, no shoes on, and, obviously, they had been walking around all day because their feet were black and streaked with dirt.

I had just sat down, when one of the girls came up to me and asked me for my ice cream.

I'm so embarrassed to admit this, but I abruptly said, "No." Then I sat down and proceeded to eat the ice cream, while the little girls watched me from afar.

As I lay in bed that night, I kept seeing her face, and the sorrowful look she gave me. It tore my heart in half. I wished I had given my ice cream to her. *How could I be so selfish, insensitive, and cold?*

It made no sense. How could I spend all those weeks selflessly working with those children in the orphanage, and in that one moment, act completely differently? Another part of myself had come out, and I was hypocritical instead. I never forgave myself for not taking that opportunity to do something good, giving them that one jubilant. Even today, there are certain songs that will trigger the memory of those girls, and their desperate and tender little faces will appear in my mind.

I didn't want this feeling to get the best of me or taint the time I had left to spend in Argentina. I knew I had to try something different. The next evening as I was walking back to the hostel, I got my chance.

On every corner of the promenade, where the cross streets were, there were always groups of men or women looking to call you into the brothels or clubs. That night was no different. As I made my way through the intersection, a woman came up to me very aggressively.

I held my hand up and firmly repeated, "No, no, no."

After seeing how serious I was, without a word, she went back to her corner.

Feeling dejected, I walked over to one of the shops, sat down at a table and ordered a coffee. From my table, I sat and watched her, as I was curious to know who she was beyond what I first saw. She was leaning against the side of a building, arms crossed, standing in the shadows. **Suddenly, I wondered if I could learn something about her that I didn't see before.** I thought, *where did she come from? How did she get here?* By the time I had nearly finished my coffee, I began to rephrase the question, *what is her gift? What makes her beautiful?* Then she turned her face in the light and I caught something in her eyes. I could see her as a child, innocent and free from all her burdens and worries.

Feeling liberated, I swiftly stood up from my chair and cleaned up my table. Then I went into the adjacent shop, bought a dozen roses, and walked over to her.

I don't know why I bought her roses, and not food, or water, or a doughnut. I just felt she needed to be recognized as a beautiful woman on the inside, regardless of what she was doing on the outside. And I wanted to do it with respect, not by saying something cliché like "you're beautiful." Obviously, what everyone else was giving her wasn't working. Somewhere hidden deep inside her was a soul, and I chose to honor it with a dozen roses.

At first, she gave me a look like, "Oh, this one changed his mind." She ignored the roses and gestured for me to go inside and "see the girls." But I looked her firmly in the eyes, determined to catch the beauty I had witnessed just moments ago. Suddenly, her shoulders dropped, and she grew quiet. There was a stillness, as if everything had stopped all around us. In that moment, I didn't see the annoying street person anymore, I saw someone's daughter, a woman who deserved to be loved - honestly, standing right in front of me.

Ceremoniously, I lifted up the bouquet of roses and handed them to her, as if she were the only woman who mattered in the world. I said, "These are for you, as you are a gift and even more beautiful then these flowers."

She was shocked.

When I saw her reaction, my heart jump-started to life again. In that moment, seeing her light up from the inside was more important than my first kiss, or even my first crush, it was so beautiful to both of us.

After this and pushing the devil aside, I extended my stay in Argentina. I had originally planned to stay for two weeks; I ended up staying for four.

A *"Problem"* child?

***

Having faced a few demons and finding light in the darkness, I felt I had acquired a few more tools for the journey and mission. Next, I would be volunteering at a group home in Buenos Aires for orphaned boys and girls.

The home was owned by several local Argentinian business women who had self-funded the venture and managed the house, along with a small staff of caretakers who came in and out during the day. When I walked inside, I immediately noticed the house was clean, comfortable, and well taken care of. In this small group home, the children had access to counselors, doctors, and schools. They had everything that a young child needs, besides their own parents.

From what I could see, the children also got along well with each other. The house was co-ed, but it was mostly girls, and out of the twelve, only two were boys, both around ten years of age. The oldest girl was eighteen, and the youngest was eleven years old. Unlike the larger orphanages, this one was more homelike. These children lived here permanently, and even though they had come from backgrounds not much different than the kids in the big institutions, it felt more like a family.

I had a lot of fun working with these children. Being inside a less rigid structure and not bombarded with hundreds of kids allowed me to get to know each child better. They were all so spirited and unique.

They spoke to me in Spanish at great length and with much seriousness, as if I understood them. As I listened to each one without interrupting them, I would think, *This one is going to use his gentle sense of courtesy, patience, and awareness to be an influential peacemaker or leader,* or *This energetic one is going to find some creative way to do great things in the world someday.*

I wasn't paying attention to their words, as much as their overall demeanor and expression. **As a result, I was able to see each and every unique glowing characteristic and emotion as they were revealed to me with every second.**

I was probably the only adult they'd encountered who wouldn't cut them off mid-sentence or correct them. They must have been thinking, *This guy can listen forever!*

I was continually amazed at how polite and well-mannered they were. One night, I decided to take them all out for McDonald's and to the movies. I was pleasantly surprised at how appropriate they acted in public. When the bus came to pick them up, without a word, they all got on one after the other and sat quietly next to one another, courteous yet elated. At McDonald's, I asked them what they each wanted, and they told me to order whatever I wanted for them; they'd be happy with it. They weren't whining or saying, "I want this," or, "I want that," like I expected. Later, we had to walk a couple blocks through a busy shopping center to get to the theater, and, again, they all stuck together. They weren't running around asking for things. We watched the Disney movie *Cars*, and I bought them buckets of popcorn and different kinds of drinks. After the movie, when the lights came on, I was surprised that they'd left most of it untouched. It blew my mind; not all of them wanted the snacks.

These children were miles above most kids their age in terms of behavior, and the caregivers did an impressive job caring for them and raising them, but I was told there were a few in the group who had stood out even more. One girl in particular was considered, for lack of a better word, a "problem." The staff warned me that she was very hyper and might hit or scratch me. I noticed her right away. She was tall for her age with a clever smile and dark hair. She was always the most active one in the room with a blur of arms and legs always in motion and seemingly couldn't sit still for any amount of time.

Normally, this type of child would annoy me, but, for some reason, I gravitated toward her immediately. I connected with something in her that I couldn't verbalize. For some reason, I knew that her "personality" was temporary, and she wasn't a hyper or aggressive person at all.

Maybe because I had experienced something similar when I was a child.

When I was 7-years-old, I heard my mother and father having a big fight. My mom came into the bedroom, grabbed me and my brother out of bed, and said, "We're going." My brother was 4 at the time. I remember my mother frantically cramming her clothes into a suitcase, screaming at my father. **Before I knew it, we were outside. It was 1am, we had no shoes on, and it was pouring rain; my pajama bottoms were soaked.** I remember looking out the back window of the yellow taxi as we drove away and seeing my father standing in the street screaming in pain, "Please... please... Don't take my boys."

After that day, I always carried a small fistful of anger like a grenade, ready at my disposal. Living at a women's shelter with my mother was extremely difficult, and my relationship with her started to fall apart. I would beg her to let me go live with my father. I even tried not bathing for a month to get her to send me to my dad's. During this time, I increasingly told her I hated her; it felt like a million times. I just wanted her to feel the shooting pain that was suffocating my heart. She sent me to a psychologist to figure out what was wrong with me, but the counseling didn't help, and my mother and I started getting into physical fights. I would pull her hair or shove her, and in her fierce self-defense, she would respond in equal measure, physically. This continued until I was about 10 or 11 years old.

Somehow, if I could yell at my mother or hit her, in a weird way, I also would still feel connected to her, as, at times, I felt completely ignored and misunderstood. And that was the root of the problem. I was tired of people trying to fix me; I just wanted to be loved. My mother told me repeatedly that she loved me, but I didn't believe her. I wanted to trust her and feel safe first.

I knew this little girl didn't feel safe, either. I could feel it. That's what I understood about her the second I saw her. I could say, "you are loved," or "I love you" to her, but she wouldn't have believed it; she also had to trust me first.

I resolved to taking every bit of abuse; she could throw anything she wanted at me, bite me, scratch me, and I wouldn't yell or get angry at her. I would just wait patiently for her to let go of the anger. Every time she came up and hit or scratched me, instead of getting angry, I thought, *Why does she want my attention?*

I knew if I responded with negative energy, she would only escalate the aggression, until one of us gave up. Like the woman chasing me down in the street, I could yell or threaten, but it wouldn't solve the negative energy and only continue the retaliation cycle. I decided to take a different approach. **Every time she hit, scratched, or bit me, I would gently touch the top of her head.** I just softly touched her in a loving way, in the safest place to touch her, and looked directly into her eyes with my heart and full attention and smiled, while mustering up as much patience and pain tolerance as I could in the moment.

This was the only way I could treat her the same as I did all the other children.

I didn't want to raise my voice or grab her like the others would by the shoulders. I wanted her to give me all her negative energy and filter it through what I saw in her, which wasn't negative at all. I wasn't going to bounce that energy back to her. I was going to change the color of it and let her see her own calm beauty through my eyes. After about a week of this, I noticed a change.

One day, she came up to me as I was filming with my camera and was talking into the lens, giggling and being silly. I noticed she kept a polite distance. Normally, she was always jumping up and down, waving her hands in people's faces, constantly tapping on things like the furniture, or your shoulder, or your arm, trying to get your attention. There was something different about her this time. I realized she had stopped hitting me. In fact, she'd stopped hitting everyone.

Finally, I thought. Her real character had revealed itself. **She wasn't a "problem" child, she was just a child with a solvable problem.**

Children don't need someone to treat them like a broken toy that needs to be fixed. They don't always need adults yelling at them or punishing them. If you want to help them change, first they have to trust, and trust takes time. It was here in this tiny orphanage in Argentina, watching this little girl blossom into a sweet and lovable child, that I finally felt I had the answer to the question, the catalyst that started my journey, *What is the one thing that all children need to have a better life?*

They just need to be loved and truly believe they are someone important in this life.

One afternoon, we were sitting at the table just after snack time. It was my last day at this group home before leaving for my next destination and I really didn't want to leave the kids, we'd had so much fun together. As I sat there, looking around the table with my translator by my side, I decided to tell them a story that I hoped would change their lives for the better.

They sat quietly in their chairs, waiting for me to speak.

I started by telling them this was a true story about a boy their age who also lived in foster care, just like them. I looked around at the expression on their faces; I had their full attention.

Sometimes, I said, the little boy also lived in parks, had a really hard time understanding his schoolwork, and didn't know why he fought with his mom so much. One time, he was even touched by his babysitter in a way that made him even more confused, withdrawn, and scared. Sometimes, I continued, he would even steal things so when he went to school, he'd have pencils and books.

I looked at one of the boys at the table, "What do you think happened to this boy?"

With a sad face, he said, "I don't know."

Another boy at the table asked, "Erik, did he become a magician?"

I smiled. "Well, I suppose so... I think we're all magicians, Carlos."

The children opened their eyes wider and sat up in their chairs. This concept seemed to interest them.

It gave me an idea; I decided to give the story a little twist. I told them this young boy took all the difficult ingredients from his life and started to make the most magical potions, not only to help himself, but others too. "Most importantly," I said, **"As the boy grew older, he realized that all his experiences, even the hurtful, difficult, and painful ones, were all a gift, a gift of understanding and of a greater meaning."**

The great thing about it was that those ingredients and recipes that are given to us as we're growing up, aren't created by us. So, you can replace them at any time. I said, "You may find those recipes no longer work anymore, and some of them are boring, outdated, or even poisonous!"

Then I asked the children, "Why would someone keep eating the same bad tasting cake they've tried before?"

"Because they're using the same recipe?" one of the girls said.

I smiled and said, "You're absolutely right!"

I told them that there were so many different ingredients in our lives, that we have the opportunity to either keep the old ones, transform them, or add new ones. There's no shortage of different options, and we can experiment with a new recipe each day!

Feeling inspired, I stood up and grabbed a spoon off the table and held it in front of them. I looked around at the table and asked, "Who here would put worms in their cookies?"

"Yuck!" they all shouted, wrinkling their noses in disgust.

When they'd calmed down, I said, "But what if when you were growing up, you saw everyone else around you put worms in their cookies?"

"That's silly," they said.

"I agree, it's silly," I told them. "But maybe some people have only ever seen grownups mixing worms into their cookies, and so they thought this was the only way to make them."

"Sometimes grownups repeat only what they saw others do, even if it's wrong or makes them sick. But I think you've all seen enough and smart enough to know what's wrong for you and others right?"

I let the kids think about this for a moment.

"Do you know the greatest advantage that you all have right now?" I asked. "Everyone knows that worms in cookies is just silly, right? So, what other great ingredients can you think of to replace those slimy, silly worms with? Can we try love and sprinkles... or caring and candy canes... or how about curiosity and chocolate chips?"

They howled with laughter.

"It's really fun when you know you have a choice isn't it?" I added.

"So, what happened to the boy?" one of the girls asked.

I told them the boy learned he was the owner of a mixing bowl (his mind), and if someone tried to put a bad ingredient into his bowl, like worms, he would replace it with something healthy that was good for him and others.

I held the spoon in my hand, and solemnly said, "He guarded the gates of his mind and his heart with a very powerful shiny spoon, taking out the things he didn't like. Now this boy is all grown up, and he still owns this shiny spoon. And he's standing right in front of you!"

The children roared with laughter.

I think I got my message across, though. The young magician, of course, was me, and like the little boy in the story, they could also be the protectors of their thoughts and creators of their own future. No matter what your past experiences, once you appreciate both the good and bad, you can start the process of change.

This small orphanage in Buenos Aires really took hold of my heart and forever expanded my perspective. I really wanted to support this organization after I left. Whether that was through my company, or financially, or some other way, I had to help these kids. I spent my last night in the group home standing in the kitchen talking with the staff and the owners, asking them about their needs and concerns. I promised to stay in touch with them after I left; we'd figure something out.

For a few months, we did stay in touch. We wrote emails to each other every month, and the staff gave me updates on the kids. But eventually it got harder to reach them, and the spaces between their emails became longer. One day, I found out they'd closed. I tried to reach out and find out what had happened to the children but was unsuccessful. Whenever I thought of this little group home, I felt sad, and I always wondered where those children went and how they were taken care of. Later, I learned what happened so often to young girls once they become of age in Latin America, and I prayed that none of them fell into that life.

Global Beliefs

***

Living at the hostel for an entire month, I could feel myself starting to pick away at my emotional shell and expose more of who I was under that old protective layer. It became easier to socialize as I started focusing on what makes others unique versus what they would think of me, and this grew beyond what I was learning being with the children and NGO leaders.

One night, I went back to the hostel around dinner time and noticed some new people sitting in the common area. One was a really tall blond man with a weathered but lively face and an Australian accent. He must have been in his fifties or sixties, but he had that piping energy of someone in their twenties, with a magnetic zest for life. He was sitting on the couch with his teenage son, they were both extremely slender, with long scraggly hair past their shoulders; they looked like a father and son surfing team. To this day, I can see their welcoming eyes and spirited expressions.

Later that week, I saw them at the bar, chatting with Marianne, my friend from New York. I had been spending my days around people who didn't speak English, so I always enjoyed the opportunity to listen to people speak, with the simple pleasure of understanding what they were saying. I pulled up a stool and had a beer or two with them (which, as you may know by now, was a stretch for me in more ways than one).

I was fascinated by the father's energy, how he carried himself and the way he spoke about the world in such a whimsical and engaging light. He described his life back home in a multitude of colors and dimensions. I learned he was a farmer in Australia with an abundance of land and crops. He loved farming. He wasn't bragging or trying to impress anybody; it was hard to describe his demeanor, but he was just incredibly genuine and captivating. **Their joy and positivity was brilliantly alive; you couldn't help wanting to be around them!**

Most people have a broad set of beliefs they use to describe their life, work, or relationships. Conscious of them or not, these "global beliefs" either bring us closer to what we want or move us farther away from it. For example, a person who has the global belief that "I have to work to live" may struggle to survive or overwork to get ahead. But someone who's more optimistic and says, "I will either do what I love or find a way to love what I do," will always try to seek the best in most situations.

Whenever I found someone with an extraordinary way of experiencing life, be it professionally or emotionally, I found myself wondering about their global beliefs. **What are their rules? How do they see the world?**

I thought, *This guy is always happy. Why don't I ask him what his rules are for being happy?*

Waiting for a pause in the conversation, I asked, "Mark, if I were to ask you what life is about in one word, what would it be?"

With a big grin on his face he said, "That's easy—it's fun." Then he smacked his hand on the bar top and declared, **"Mate, if it's not fun, I don't do it!"**

I sat quietly, reflecting on his words, shook his hand, and said, "Thank you."

Sometimes, I made my life far too complicated when the answers are so simple. "It's nice to find someone who didn't overcomplicate things," I added.

On my last weekend in Buenos Aires, Maríanne and I spent time touring the city. One day, we were walking by the Obelisk, and turned down a wide thoroughfare. It was a major avenue with shops and apartments on one side and a large green park on the other side.

As we were walking south, on the left-hand side near the shops, I noticed a tall slender lady with long black hair tied back, wearing dirty oversized clothing and broken sandals standing in the alleyway between the buildings. I could see she had a baby in her arms. Ahead of me on the sidewalk, I saw an American couple, walking with a big paper map in their hands. With their brightly colored cheap baseball caps and fanny packs, they stuck out like sore thumbs. I immediately realized who the woman in the alley was staring at in anticipation.

She saw them, but they didn't see her.

I watched her rocking her baby back and forth, she seemed agitated. As the couple got closer, she pulled the little red blanket off its face, lifted her hand up above her head, and in the darkness by the edge of the alleyway, she slapped the tiny baby sweepingly across the face, hard. You could hear it from where I was standing. **I stopped Maríanne, grabbed her hand firmly, and pulled down, to anchor both of us. I said, "Wait, wait."**

It took a few seconds for the baby to start crying after she slapped it. Then we heard a throaty howl from the child.

The American couple looked up from their map with concern, as the woman came running out of the alleyway toward them, saying, "Por favor, por favor… baby hungry, baby hungry."

The baby was crying and screaming of course.

The couple opened their fanny packs and gave her some money, and just as swiftly as she had appeared, the woman vanished with her baby back into the alleyway. I was beyond angry.

The sense of personal triumph and the positive mindset I had so carefully cultivated over the past few days evaporated instantly. I thought,

There's too much darkness here, too much poverty. This place is corrupt! And now mothers are hitting their own newborns for money?

I had to control myself. I felt like running after her, pointing my finger in her face and accusing her of child abuse. Rather than going after this woman or doing something stupid, I took a second to calm down. I stood there for a few minutes on the sidewalk with my eyes shut, just focusing on my breath. **Suddenly, a voice came into my head, I remembered reading somewhere that** *people do the best with what they know.*

That was it. Maybe this mother only knew one way to feed herself and her child. She felt it was the only way, and she was doing the best with what she knew. Then, I remembered something else, another, quieter voice told me, *Sometimes, people will violate their values to meet their basic human needs.*

I had compassion for her because I didn't know what it was like being a mother. I didn't know the other 99% of what she dealt with, or the life experiences that took her to that place at that specific moment. But it was a titanic struggle. I had to use every ounce of my energy to not judge her and try to see the situation from a place of understanding.

This wasn't the way I imagined ending my trip to Argentina. The city had offered some bright moments but also a lot of darkness to work through.

On one hand, I was able to connect with people I wouldn't normally associate with in an entirely new way, without trying to prove myself, or worrying about being "enough." I had even arrived at a place where I could go beyond words, see the person on a deep level, understand them, and connect with them a little more than I would ever before. It was a transcendent lesson for me. I learned how to be present with people and give them my undivided and genuine attention without expectation of who someone is or should be. This opened me up to new discoveries and an appreciation for what I saw hidden within them.

Whether it was sharing a simple moment with the nuns in the garden, playing gently with the orphans in the group home, or having a beer with my fellow travelers, I wasn't pretending to be anyone else, overcompensating, or explaining who I was. **As a result, I could begin to see who they really were and allow myself to truly feel connected and fulfilled as I shared moments and laughter with them.**

Even though Argentina had given me so much, helping me figure out a way to bring light into the darkest places and to even love and appreciate some of my angry moments, I decided it was time for a break. My next country, I wouldn't be volunteering, interviewing, or working at all. I booked a room at a small resort hotel on the beach in Uruguay for a week. I wanted to take some time for myself, to reflect on the journey, and the lessons, and what I still had to uncover thus far.

Uruguay:
Finding Purpose in...

June 2006
Punta del Este, Uruguay

***

B oarding the boat, I was thankful and amazed at how modern and luxurious it was. I made my way up the spiral staircase to the first-class seating on the top level, and saw a big open area, with chairs and small tables arranged like a flat movie theater. You could walk around comfortably and get food and drinks from the snack bar. I'd never been on something that was a cross between a ferry and a cruise ship before, so this was a enthralling experience.

I chose a seat near the railing of the boat and looked out over the dark blue-gray waves of the Atlantic. In a few hours, we would arrive in Punta del Este, known as the "St. Tropez" of South America, a resort town in Uruguay where many wealthy Argentines (and, of course, Uruguayans) had their vacation homes.

By this point, I was ready for some down time after all those days I spent focusing my attention on the children and the directors of the organizations I'd interviewed and volunteered at. I had never focused on anything so intensely and with such great purpose before. My goal for this short break was to simply sit in a quiet place and think about all the special things I'd seen, unpack my experiences, and review my notes. Then I could review what was working and what wasn't for each organization, what their strengths were, and how I perceived the quality of life of these children in each situation.

As I was deep in thought, looking out over the horizon, I heard a deep and friendly voice close to me say, "Hola," and I was pulled out of my thoughts.

I turned to look at the man sitting next to me who had said hello. He was a well-to-do older gentleman, probably in his seventies, dressed very sharply, wearing a sort of casual smart blazer with a scarf. Even though he was "rich in age," his gestures were animated and lively, which gave him a youthful air. He spoke fluent English with a sharp and elegant Argentine accent and seemed keen on having a conversation with me. For the next half an hour, we talked about life, relationships (ex-wives), our favorite music, and the difference between Argentina and Uruguay.

During our lively conversation, I asked him the reason for his visit to Uruguay. With a little half smile and a sparkle in his eye, he tilted his head and said, "I'm going to see my girlfriend."

That's really nice, I thought! *He's probably a widower, just getting back out there on the dating scene.* It piqued my curiosity, so I said, "Tell me more about her."

"We get along very well... we play cards, drink wine, take walks, and, most importantly, we enjoy each other's company," he said. "With that, I visit her every month or so."

I came to learn later on, in between his escapades in Uruguay, he goes back home to Argentina to take care of his responsibilities and spend time with his wife of fifty years.

That conversation took a turn I hadn't expected.

With a contented smile and a tap of his hand on my knee, he told me he wanted to take a nap before his big weekend and our conversation came to an end. I sat back in my seat with a smile, thinking about my new friend sneaking off like a mischievous little boy to see his sweetheart; he was a man seeking love, unaware that his "home" is probably seeking it as well. We relaxed in silence for the rest of the trip. As the ferry approached the shore, I saw gleaming white and gray buildings along the port. After disembarking I would take a *Buque Bus* to Montevideo, the capital of Uruguay, and then a cab to my hotel in Punta del Este. I got off the boat feeling refreshed from the short sea journey, and eager to start my break so I could further reflect and process.

Day One: The Sound of Silence

***

"Holding on is believing that there's only a past;

letting go is knowing that there's a future."

—Daphne Rose Kingma

Arriving in Punta del Este during the winter months was an unexpected gift. Not only was everything within a mile radius closed, apparently, I was the only guest in the entire beachfront boutique hotel.

When we pulled up, I hesitated to get out of the cab. The hotel looked closed.

On first sight, the hotel reminded me of a ranch home with two levels, very wide, and no more than 10 rooms. The grounds were surrounded by large shady trees, and on the other side was the beach. I'd picked it online because the style of the main building with its white walls, structural wood accents, and sloping roof, nestled in greenery all around looked cozy and reminded me a little of the house I had just sold.

I scanned the property for signs of life. No cars were in the driveway, and I couldn't see any staff on the grounds, nothing.

Although the hotel was in an affluent neighborhood, surrounded by stunning cottage style vacation homes, I would soon come to learn that 99% of them were empty. In fact, the town was so desolate, during the ride I asked my driver if it was abandoned. Equally confused, my driver couldn't understand why anyone would visit Punta del Este in the winter time. He repeatedly asked me questions about my trip, but when I answered, he just scratched his head and shrugged.

Looking at the place I'd be staying for the next week, I thought, *Now I know why the hotel was so cheap!* I'd booked it during their off season.

Reluctantly, I paid the fare. The long taxi ride from Montevideo to Punta cost me a small fortune, so I knew I wasn't going back into town, unless absolutely necessary. Once I got out of the cab, there was no going back, until my stay was over.

Through the open reception area of the hotel, you could see the bluish band of the ocean over the green grass. A cold breeze blew off the water and cut through my thin t-shirt. It was only 57 degrees, but, somehow, I found it refreshing. Nobody was at the desk to greet me, I had to walk around the grounds looking for someone to help me check in. Luckily, the owner and his wife lived on site and there were one or two general maintenance people on staff even during the off season. The owner kindly informed me that although breakfast would be served in my room every morning, I was on my own for lunch and dinner, as the hotel restaurant was closed during the winter months. In that moment, I wasn't quite sure how I was going to feed myself, but I was confident I would figure it out one way or another. Surely, there had to be some food close by.

Once I saw my room, any doubts or reservations I'd had vanished. It was extremely cozy, with warm earthy orange stucco walls and a fireplace at the end of a large wooden bed. I immediately threw my backpack in the corner and went out onto the balcony to look at the ocean. It was very rustic, nothing fancy, but I felt totally at home.

A few minutes later, I made myself a blazing fire in the fireplace, and sat on the corner of the bed, warming my hands a bit. **I thought, *Okay, I'm here. What's next?***

This was the only country I'd visited where I had no agenda.

Pulling my backpack toward me, I took out my 12" laptop, iPod, headphones, and stacks of notes from the interviews I had conducted at the orphanages. I also took out the plans for the next business I was building. Then I spread it all out on the crocheted blanket on top of the bed, and looked down at this sea of notebooks, electronic devices, and sheets of paper around me.

After a few moments of taking it all in, I said out loud, "This is crazy."

Growth doesn't happen in comfort and certainty, if you do what you've always done, you'll always get similar results. I had to do things differently. I thought, *What if I take this time to really learn something new?*

First, I closed my laptop and put it back in the bag. Then I took my notes and closed them and put them away. The TV was already on, so I grabbed the remote and turned it off. *It's all just noise and distractions anyway,* I thought.

Finally, I threw my backpack down on the floor and laid back on the bed. For the remainder of the trip, I told myself, no writing, no planning, no computer, no emails, no music, no reading, no TV, nothing would distract me from silence and being 100% present in the moment or take me from the relentless processing of my own thoughts.

Restlessly, I stretched out on top of the bed, attempting to relax while listening to the crackle of the fire. Out of habit, I reached for my iPod. I propped myself up with pillows and put my knees up and my headphones on. Then I realized I had already broken my rule of no music.

You can't listen to music anymore during this time, I told myself.

After briefly arguing with myself in my head, I reluctantly put the iPod away. Then I started thinking about Diana. My mind was going everywhere, back and forth, like a game of ping pong. Finally, I got up, and sat on the edge of the bed, with my hands between my legs, one on top of the other. I had my feet crossed, my legs were twitching, and I was nervously bouncing up and down. It was very unlike me.

This is interesting, I thought. It was almost like withdrawals. I wondered if I was like this after just a few minutes, what was going to happen after a few hours? Or a few days?

Then I remembered a time when my ex-wife and I had tried to not watch TV at all after hearing someone say it was an "income reducer." The point was instead of watching someone else's life on television, live more of your own life. It was our little experiment. The first couple of nights, we couldn't figure out what to do with ourselves. So, we went to bed at 8pm every night for about a week, until we couldn't stand it any longer and started to find more enjoyable and productive things to do with our evenings, such as reading books, taking walks, and even talking to each other.

I thought with amusement, *If I could survive that, I can do this.*

I sat there in silence, determined. **The first few minutes were really aggravating and the first hour felt like a week.** I slowly and unconsciously paced circles around the room, stared at the paintings on the walls, counted the number of stones in each painting, then walked to the bathroom and counted the tiles. It was really funny. Normally, I'm not a playful person, but over the next 24 hours, I found myself becoming playful and acting like a little kid (who's really bored). From that perspective, everything was new and vivid and undiscovered.

Then I had a really crazy thought: *What if I don't talk to anyone?*

No, that was too much, I decided. Making phone calls and using the Internet to communicate was okay, but then I decided to put that on pause as well, and truly commit to this silence and avoidance of distraction.

Something snapped me out of my playful mood, my stomach was growling. Since I had arrived at the hotel just before lunch, I hadn't noticed it right away. Now, I realized I'd have to go find some food shortly or go to bed hungry. At the front desk, I had to break my vow of silence to ask the staff where the closest grocery store was.

"It's a two-hour walk," they said, in broken English.

Smiling, I said, "Point me in the direction."

The grocery store was in the same general direction as the town, so I decided to walk along the beach. I didn't mind the long walk, I was used to it, and it allowed me to kill some time. Plus, walking in the sand was an added bonus, enjoying the sights and sounds of the sea, while getting a bit more exercise as I balanced myself with each step along the shore.

The beach was entirely empty, just sand and crashing waves. As I made my way down some wooden steps and onto the sand, it took a few moments to adjust, but then my mind became exceptionally clear. I saw things in my surroundings that I wouldn't normally notice, like colored stones and shells and different types of birds that were playing in the surf or fishing in the water. **As I walked, my mental focus increased, and I even got to the point where I was able to prevent myself from projecting my thoughts into the**

past or the future. For instance, I might see a charming beach house and think, "That would be a really nice home to have." I could almost imagine a family spending time out on the porch, with multiple generations enjoying life and making new treasured memories together. And then, just like that I'd be interrupted with thoughts about my business, my future, and money. Instead, I forced myself not to go beyond what I was seeing in the moment. It was an intriguing and animated exercise, for sure.

Finally, I saw the grocery store, but it wasn't a grocery store at all. It was a convenience store, more like a 7-11. Still, I managed to purchase the basics, some bread, cheese, and ham, enough to make sandwiches. Then, once I had my "rations" for the next 24 to 48 hours, all snug in one small gray plastic bag, I proceeded to walk two hours back to my hotel with both my lunch and dinner in my hands.

The walk along the beach was lonely and liberating at the same time. There wasn't a single soul in sight, it was the first time I'd ever experienced anything like it. By the time I arrived at the hotel my hands were numb. For a Canadian, it wasn't cold to the point of being unbearable, but even with a t-shirt and a sweater, it was pretty chilly. Inside the room, I hung my socks by the fireplace to dry and hungrily ate my ham and cheese sandwich. I had a long week ahead of me, yet I went to bed feeling strangely triumphant. The point is, I survived day one.

Day Two
✳✳✳

I was awakened by a gentle knock at the door. I stumbled out of bed and found a woman standing outside with a breakfast tray. She glanced at me with a worried look; it occurred to me that the owners probably felt sorry for me being all alone here. I said *gracias* and took the tray inside my room. Breakfast was bread and cheese, which didn't help much, since I already had bread and cheese, but I was thankful and thanked them kindly. I sat the tray on the corner of my bed and walked toward the balcony doors opposite the bed.

Upon opening the door to the balcony, I noticed the air was a bit colder than the day before. I pulled my Irish wool sweater on over my t-shirt and prepared to go out for my daily walk along the beach. I wanted to take the time to stroll and be with my thoughts and potentially discover something new in the silence. If I had stayed in the room all day, I knew I'd go stir crazy (or stuff myself with bread and cheese out of boredom).

As I retraced my steps from the previous day, I couldn't help but reflect on the experiences I had on my trip so far. It almost seemed as if they were overlapped with what was happening in front of me on the beach. I saw the children's faces in the waves and the sand. Eventually, even those images disappeared into the silence, and I started thinking, *If I can't distract myself, then how can I entertain myself?*

I don't typically play sports, but suddenly I wanted to play. Never had I had such a strong desire to be physical, not even when I was a kid. **It occurred to me that there was no one to play with, just my imagination.** So, I proceeded to pretend that the beach was my own private amusement park and I was the only one there. I never went into anyone's house, but I wandered around the various beachfront properties around the hotel. Some of the homes had jungle gyms and kid's forts in their backyards. In one yard, I slid down the slide, and played hide and go seek with myself. Then, I found a see-saw, and sat down on it as if someone were on the other side.

I was having the most ridiculous conversations with myself the whole time. I literally found a lightbulb on the ground, picked it up, put it on my head, and thought, *I could come up with a great idea today!* At one point, I found myself on the grounds of a house with a security alarm sign in the window. I thought, *This is interesting. Maybe I shouldn't be trespassing.*

In retrospect, my behavior was a little bizarre, but I didn't care because it was a ghost town. There was no one to see me taking silly photos of myself or sitting in front of a restaurant looking at my imaginary watch, wondering when the waiter would come to take my order (it was empty). I didn't know what the purpose of all this was, and maybe there wasn't a purpose. **Truly, for the first time I had zero worries, zero anxiety, and no plans for the future or wonder about what tomorrow would bring.** I wasn't wondering "who will love me," or "will I be okay?" Once I had cleared all the distractions out, my childlike spirit, my joy, could finally express itself.

Maybe my inner child just figured out that there wasn't anything to be distracted by or worried about—no future, no past—and decided it was safe to come out and play.

After my day of fun (and another ham and cheese sandwich), I lay down in bed, exhausted but truly joyous.

Day Three: Who's There?

✳✳✳

The sand and sea stretched out for miles, filling my field of vision all the way to the horizon. To my right, the waves crashed and pummeled the shore; overhead, seabirds circled noisily. The sky was overcast and gray, which reflected my subdued mood that day. Almost in a meditative state, taking notice of every single step I made in the sand, every passing breeze, I bent down and pulled my sneakers off, so I could feel every part of my foot—heel, arch, toes—snuggling into the sand. I was headed to the store to get my daily ration of bread and cheese (maybe some jam if I was lucky).

It had taken me three days to get used to the enforced silence. Being connected to my inner world, rather than being distracted by the outer world, I felt extraordinarily light. **I felt a sense of peacefulness in me that wasn't**

forced or based on what I owned or achieved. This, I felt, was real happiness, the opposite of what my dad had been talking about when he warned me years ago about the pitfalls of temporary happiness. Only, he told me at the height of my material wealth, so I didn't understand at the time. Now I did.

As I walked, I found myself in an unusual state of mental calm. The fighting had stopped in my head. I didn't have to actively suppress the urge to think about the past or the future. I was immersed in the moment, aware of every grain of sand between my toes, the smell of the ocean, the sound of the bird's wings clapping above me. All my senses were on high alert.

Coming back from the store, about halfway through, I felt something inside me let go even more. I continued to open up to what was going on around me, until I felt something unusual happening. Now I know this is going to sound strange or overly spiritual to some, and even I look back on this experience with plenty of unanswered questions. This is a moment that I'll never forget, and I wish that everyone could experience it at least once in their life. At one point, I felt that I was nothing and everything at the same time. I was part of the ocean, I was part of the breeze, the fish—everything. It was a sublime moment of peacefulness, without concern or worry, yet I had an intuitive understanding of how everything was feeling around me. **As soon as tried to logically examine what was happening, the connection and whole experience came to a halt.**

How did I do it?

I was so excited, I started retracing my steps in my mind, thinking, *How did it happen?* As I evaluated the process, the second I started thinking consciously about it, my connection to my surroundings started to dissipate. I ended up desperately trying to hold onto that feeling, as it slipped elusively away.

As I stood there in the sand, facing the ocean, acutely aware of my own internal struggle, I distinctly heard a voice say, "You have to help them heal."

I thought, *Where is this coming from?*

No answer.

I spun around, arms wide open, saying, "How? What do you mean? Who do I heal? Everybody?"

I stared at the empty beach and listened for the answer. Nothing.

I still had so many unanswered questions, I thought maybe if I could get back to that state, I could find the answers. But the voice and that feeling were gone. After a few moments of waiting for something to happen, I gave up and started making my way down the beach again, headed back to the hotel.

It was like someone had flipped a switch in my brain, and everything went from positive to negative. I was probably only a half hour away from the hotel, when suddenly I started noticing things I'd never noticed before. Garbage, everywhere. I hadn't seen all the plastic bags, bottles, and countless condoms, seven or eight of them, embedded in the sand. I put my sneakers back on in disgust, the beach was filthy.

How had I missed all this trash? The first few days of my trip I was so focused on letting go, I hadn't even seen it!

There was an interesting correlation between my conscious thoughts and what I chose to see in my surroundings. I was convinced that if I had continued opening myself up even more, I'd have also continued seeing the amazing things around me. And when I closed myself off again, the beach looked dirty.

Now I was even more convinced that I could reach that special state I had experienced earlier on command. I tried to control my thoughts; in fact,

I practiced meditating diligently for the rest of the week, but I was never able to get it back one hundred percent again.

I still had three more days, but I don't remember much after that. On the last day in Punta del Este, I went back to that same section of the beach and said a quiet thank you to the sand and the ocean. For some reason it felt like family to me. I paced back and forth under the bright blue sky expressing my gratitude silently for twenty minutes or more, it was a very long thank you, I don't think I've thanked anyone or anything in my life as much as I thanked that place.

My vacation in Punta del Este had been surprisingly insightful, and I couldn't wait to get back home to start writing about it. What a powerful time. I didn't have enough words to express enough how incredible it was taking a break from the noise and chatter of my everyday life and going through that experience. It reminded me of a saying, "Why do angels fly? Because they take themselves lightly."

I am definitely not an angel, but I certainly ascended for a short while.

Finding Purpose
***

We must be willing to let go of the life we've planned,
so as to have the life that is waiting for us."
—Joseph Campbell

What is our purpose in life? What is our mission? Should it be grand and abundant, or humble, simple, and graceful? Your purpose is whatever is important to you—what fills your heart—and it isn't always a straight line from A to B. The problem is, how do we find out what it is? How do we discover it?

What if you were told that you'll never find it by adding things to your life? Why? From experience, it's not something that can be found in our outside world; it's something that finds you if you're willing to listen.

It reminds me of the story of the Zen master and the academic I heard from Dr. Wayne Dyer.

A university professor went to visit a famous Zen Buddhist master in the mountains of India, looking for wisdom and enlightenment. While the master quietly served tea, the professor talked about Zen. In an effort to impress his master, the professor spoke about all the great things he knew, all the books he had written on the subject, and the details he'd remembered about the Zen master's life and that of Buddha.

As he was speaking, the master filled the visitor's cup to the brim, and then kept pouring. The professor watched the overflowing cup until he could no longer restrain himself. He shouted, "You're making a mess! The cup is already full and it's spilling all over the place! No more will go in!"

"You are like this cup," the master replied with a clever smile, "You are so full of what you believe you already know, how can you possibly have room for anything new?"

This story came to mind when I left Uruguay. As I packed up my backpack and checked out of the hotel in Punta del Este, somehow, I felt like I was leaving my former self behind. I had escaped the burdens of my thoughts and distractions, and in my own way, died while I was still alive.

When we fill our attention and focus with too many empty influences and noise, we tend to lose touch with ourselves, our dreams, and our purpose. Although distractions temporarily give us comfort from the stresses of life, they also delay what we're really meant to do.

Another lesson that arose from my experiences in Uruguay was the certainty that as we grow older, the rules, responsibilities, and goals in this ever-changing environment start to drown out that inner voice. **We don't hear that part of us quietly telling us the truth anymore.** The more noise we have in our life, the less room we give ourselves to say, *This is my essence, and here's what I've been brought to this earth for; these are my brothers and sisters, and these are the gifts we all have to share.*

I swore to honor that voice as much as possible during the rest of my journey and do my best to fulfill my purpose.

Feeling fully re-energized, I eagerly made plans for the next leg of my trip. With the help of Diana, I would be visiting Colombia, the country where my girlfriend was from. But first, I had planned a short stop-over in Brazil (against Diana's wishes). She'd heard rumors about all the beautiful Brazilian women there and didn't want to take any chances. Of course, I was crazy about Diana, so she had nothing to worry about, and I wanted to see as much of Latin America as I could. I couldn't see myself skipping over the largest country on the continent. So, I booked it anyway.

Brazil and Venezuela: Nothing is What it Seems

June 2006
São Paulo, Brazil
***

A ny plans I had of seeing the unique beauty of Brazil was dashed when I saw the immigration officer's face. After twenty minutes of standing in the customs line in the Sao Paulo airport, the stern looking guard took one look at my passport and asked me to step aside.

I stood there nervous, bewildered, wondering, *Is something wrong?* From what I could tell, there seemed to be a commotion in the customs booth. The guards were hunched over my passport, passing it back and forth, and talking amongst each other. Finally, the officer handed it back to me.

"Your passport needs to be valid for six months," he said, pointing to the expiration date.

"I was unaware that this was a requirement," I replied, searching his face for signs of understanding. There was no hint of sympathy in his eyes.

"Is there anything I can do here?"

"No," he said. "We can't let you into the country at this time."

"You'll have to book a flight out of Brazil immediately, you cannot stay here at the airport," he added.

He pointed in the direction of the airline ticket counter and called the next person in line up to the desk.

"Okay," I said, walking away in shock.

What am I going to do, I wondered. I hadn't planned on this.

It wasn't easy finding a ticket agent who spoke English, but eventually I found someone willing to help me. After what felt like an hour negotiating with various airlines and desperately searching for flights, I ended up spending an astronomical amount of money on a ticket. **Unfortunately, there weren't any direct flights to Bogota, so I decided to spend a few days in Caracas, Venezuela, another country I knew next to nothing about.** Diana had warned me that there were a lot of challenges in Venezuela at that moment, especially in their relations with the U.S, but I thought, *How bad can it be?*

After the attendant gave me my ticket, I went straight to my gate. Wearily, I found a spot on the carpet in the departure area and sat down on the floor. I felt like I had been through a battle, and I wasn't certain I'd been victorious. Using my backpack as a pillow, I crossed my arms over my chest, closed my eyes, and tried to relax as much as possible. I'd be spending the next seven hours in the hallway of the airport until my flight departure time.

I just hoped that I would have more luck in Venezuela than I had in Brazil.

June 2006
Caracas, Venezuela

***

After a ten-hour flight from Sao Paulo to Caracas, I stumbled off the plane feeling stiff and sore, but happy to be on the ground.

As soon as I stepped through the arrivals gate my stomach dropped. The airport was decrepit, with outdated stained flooring, and dingy walls that looked like they hadn't seen a coat of new paint since the seventies. **Walking through the terminal, I noticed an absence of amenities, there were no restaurants, no airport bars, or brightly lit stores with tempting duty-free items that I could spot.** Just a few sparsely stocked snack stands. It reminded me of a dilapidated and forgotten bus terminal.

With a sigh, I thought, *Well, I'm here; let's get on with it.*

It was 7pm in Caracas when I arrived, and I had no hotel reservations, no Venezuelan currency, and no way to email Diana. I had been counting on there being a placard with the names of local hotels that I could call when I got there. That wasn't the case. To compound this situation, finding someone who spoke English was almost impossible.

As I stepped out of the baggage claim area, I saw a crowd of taxi drivers and hotel staff standing around with clipboards and signs in their hands, looking at the arriving passengers (most of them were locals) with great interest. I had been previously warned that some of these folks weren't always authorized drivers, and because of this, there was a much greater chance of being robbed if you accepted a ride from them, or worse. So, I kept my head down, looking for another solution. Avoiding eye contact wasn't easy, I felt like a sheep walking by a pack of hungry wolves.

The first obstacle I had to overcome was that I needed money, I knew I could figure the rest out as long as I had cash. There were some bank machines on the other side of the terminal, so I headed over to take out some money. Once I found one that looked remotely safe, I slid my debit card into the card reader, and got an error message. It wouldn't recognize my card. I moved on to the next ATM. No luck. I took my card out and went to the next machine— same story. After unsuccessfully trying four of them, I realized that none of the ATM's were going to work for my foreign bank cards.

I wasn't sure if it was because of the political conflict, but another problem was that nobody took U.S. dollars in Venezuela, not even at McDonalds (which I later learned). The realization was setting in that I couldn't use my bank card, and even if I got American dollars, it still wouldn't have worked. I glanced around, looking for some sign of what to do. Through the windows of the airport I could see night was falling fast, I had to figure something out.

Hesitantly, I walked up to one of the clipboard guys, the ones who least looked at me like fresh meat earlier. **One of them was holding a sign that said 'Paradise Hotel' with little hand painted palm trees.** I thought, *How bad can that be?*

The man immediately perked up when he saw me heading his way.

"*Hola,*" I said reluctantly.

There were about three guys standing with him and they began eagerly talking to me in Spanish all at once. I couldn't understand what they were saying, but I needed to know if they would take my money. I said, "Mastercard?"

"Yes, yes," the men said, nodding vigorously.

That was all I needed to hear.

"Okay," I said reluctantly. "Let's go."

Then something curious happened. As if I was their one and only sale for the day, they closed up the entire information booth, packed up all their backpacks and clipboards, and escorted me to the hotel van. Either it was the end of their shift, or they only needed one sale for the day. Regardless, I had a place to sleep.

The men held the van door open for me, and I tossed my backpack in the back and climbed in.

Well, I thought, *This should be enlightening to say the least.*

On the ride to the hotel I got a good look at the city, and both the beauty and the harsh reality of Venezuela. It was the first time I'd seen hollowed out buildings, burnt cars on the streets, people standing around bonfires. This was the stuff I'd seen in war torn countries in movies, but never in real life. Diana was right; there was a lot of civil unrest.

I started to worry a little bit as the part of town we were driving through was very industrial, and we seemed to be very far from the nicer parts of the city or even the suburbs. It was hard to imagine a place called "Paradise Hotel" in an area like this. **After about an hour's drive, finally, we pulled into the hotel gates, and two men armed with military grade rifles approached us to check our IDs and the van.** They were friendly enough after they saw my Canadian passport, but I wondered, *What kind of place is this?*

Inside, "Paradise Hotel" wasn't much nicer than an overgrown laundromat, just a nondescript concrete building with rooms in it, very basic. I walked over to the reception desk, which turned out to be an oversized makeshift closet with a desk in it. As I approached, the woman sitting at the desk looked up from her paperwork. Checking the nightly rate on the wall (I didn't want her thinking I was an idiot who didn't know the nightly rates), I handed her my Mastercard, which she slid through the machine to process the payment.

After the first swipe, the receptionist frowned. She took the card out and then slid it through again, this time more slowly. My neck felt hot, and I leaned over the desk in concern. After the second attempt, she finally said, "Sorry."

The machine wasn't working. *Great.*

I was starving after a ten-hour flight and desperately wanted to get out of my dirty clothes and get cleaned up. She said they would call and figure it out, so I decided to find some food in the meantime. I told the hotel clerk I would be back to check about the card after dinner. She agreed and gave me the key to my hotel room.

The same guy from the airport offered to walk me to a local restaurant. **"The neighborhood is very dangerous," he said. From what I saw earlier, I definitely believed him.**

Outside the front gates of the hotel, we walked three blocks to a local restaurant. It had an open front, with tables and chairs set out on a dark red ceramic tile floor. Above the seating area were two large-screen TV's, with soccer games playing on them. Some locals were inside eating and socializing. It reminded me of a cafeteria.

My hotel-appointed "bodyguard" sat at one of the tables down from me and ordered himself a soda. The plastic seats were sticky in the sweltering heat. I opened the menu, but I wasn't sure what to eat, so I ordered a Caesar salad, since it was one of the few items I recognized.

Thankfully, the order didn't take long to arrive, and I was quite distracted by my new surroundings. As I ate my salad, I casually glanced around the room. About eight or so customers were in the restaurant. I noticed young women at a table watching TV near the front of the restaurant. From time to time, I would look up and catch them staring at me with beautiful smiles on their faces. When I smiled back at them, they would elbow each other and look away, giggling. I thought they were cute, but other than that, I didn't think much of it.

Just as I was finishing my meal, one of the girls got up from the table and came over and gave me her phone number. She gave me a little coy smile after handing me the note and went and sat down. That had never happened to me before. Feeling pretty good about myself, I thought, *I like this country!*

Of course, I couldn't call her. I didn't even know how to make a call and couldn't speak Spanish if I did. I thought it was nice of her, and it lifted my spirits for the night.

My chaperone from the hotel paid for my meal and told me it would be added to my final bill. As we were leaving, I went over and said goodbye to the ladies. They giggled and waved as I exited the restaurant.

Now that I had some food in my stomach, I felt a bit more at peace. It was about 9pm, and I was eager to get back to the hotel so I could have a proper shower and get a good night's sleep.

As we walked back to the hotel, my guide began asking me questions in broken English. "Did you like the food?" he asked.

"Yes," I said.

"Did you like the... women?" he asked.

I smiled. "Yes," I said, remembering the girl who gave me her number.

"You want some women tonight?" he suggested.

"No, no, no," I said, holding my hand up to signal "stop."

"Okay, okay," he said.

After that, he changed the subject and began asking me about Canada and my travels. *Maybe he's trying to be my buddy or something,* I thought. No harm, but I definitely didn't want to give this guy the wrong idea about me.

When we arrived at the hotel, I discovered they had gotten the credit card machine fixed, and I said a little prayer of thanks when my card worked. Now that my credit card issue was solved, it was time to head to my hotel room and get settled in for the night. The same gentleman who had walked me to the restaurant, escorted me to my room.

As we entered the main part of the hotel, I was immediately reminded of a post-apocalyptic scenario horror movie. Am I overexaggerating? Possibly, but I'm not too far off here. **We could have been in an abandoned mental institution or hospital, with long dark hallways, thick concrete walls, and flickering electrical lights.** My room was nothing more than a small bed and a window that faced the hallway, somewhat like an oversized prison cell. It was basic and absent of any comforts, but I was too tired to care. Exhausted, I kicked my shoes off and got undressed to take a shower.

After a hot rinse, I came out of the bathroom, sat on the edge of the bed and turned on the TV. I wasn't naked, I had a towel around my waist, but I wasn't fully clothed either. Yawning, I flipped through the channels until I found what looked like a news station. Out of the corner of my eye, I saw something go by my window. It was the top of someone's head, walking by my room, quickly. All the hair stood up on my neck. *What was that?*

My eyes were glued to the window. A few seconds later, it went by again. Then, it passed by a third time, but this time more deliberately, slowly. The top of the head stopped right in front of my window.

Suddenly, I saw a hand slide through the bars on the window and beckon me.

Every muscle in my body froze. I thought, *What the fuck is that?*

Pulling the towel tighter around my waist, I slowly went up close to the window and peered through the bars. It was the same man who had walked me to my room, the one who asked me about the girls on the way back from the restaurant. The second he saw me, he leaned forward and winked. Then he said something I roughly understood as a sexual invitation.

Instinctively, I backed away from the window. "No!" I yelled.

Then I immediately closed the window and locked the door. Pulling my boxers on, hastily, I jumped into bed. I was quite freaked out by the whole thing. *Who else has the keys to my room,* I wondered? There I was, in Paradise Hotel, with armed guards outside the gates carrying machine guns. This was the first time on my trip so far I could say I was truly freaked out.

I only stayed one night. The next morning, I took a taxi to the Ramada Inn in downtown Caracas and booked a room there instead. On the way there, we drove by shopping centers and fast food restaurants, and it was far more improved, commercial area of in Caracas, but I didn't want to be there anymore. The fact that I didn't have full access to my bank account and my money, made me very nervous. Later on, at the hotel, I was relieved that I was finally able to reach Diana by phone and tell her about my experiences in Venezuela. Unsurprisingly, she encouraged me to leave as soon as possible.

Colombia was the final country on my list to visit. It seemed fitting to end my trip by visiting the place where the love of my life was born. Eagerly, the next morning I boarded my flight to Bogota, and sat down in my seat with a sense of relief. I couldn't tell if I was happy about my journey being over soon, or if I was just a bit worn out, all I knew was that I couldn't leave Venezuela—in its current political state—fast enough.

Colombia: Worth from The Heart

July 2006
Bogotá, Colombia

***

As the plane began its descent, I casually glanced out the tiny window to my right and saw the vast and stunning green landscape below me. It took me by surprise, **Colombia looked nothing like the stereotypical third-world country depicted in the movies.** From what I could see firsthand, Bogota was a modern civilization nestled in between the peaks of the Andes mountains, with a nice balance of homes, city buildings, and patches of emerald green parks.

El Dorado airport wasn't as big as I expected, but I was relieved to see there were working bank machines, restaurants, brightly lit newsstands, and many of the familiar modern conveniences you'd expect at an international airport. After splashing some water on my face in the bathroom, and stretching my back, I headed over to the baggage area on the other side of the terminal to claim my backpack from the conveyor belt.

The moment I emerged on the other side of the wall, I was greeted by a beautiful and welcoming sight, a sea of families waiting for their loved ones.

What looked like several generations, parents, grandparents, and children, were all standing there eagerly, many of them holding signs with colorful drawings and handwritten names on them. **As I stepped out from behind the partition, all eyes were on me for a brief instant.** I felt like I was a superstar, walking out onto the red carpet at the Grammys.

I'd never seen anything like this at any other airport. *Wow, families are so truly important and close here,* I thought.

Scanning the crowd, I soon spotted a sign with my name on it, and behind it were the three cheerful faces looking back at me, Diana's mother, father, and brother. Even though Diana and I had been dating for just four months (technically we'd only seen each other eight or nine times in person), her family insisted I stay with them in Bogota. I took them up on the offer, and, judging by their open expressions, they were just as curious to meet me as I was to meet them.

After a round of hugs, we managed to introduce ourselves (only the brother spoke a little English) then walked to the parking lot and squeezed into their compact Chevy car. There wasn't a lot of room, so I sat with my backpack on my lap, and theirs. As we drove through the suburbs of Bogota, I saw that Colombia was even more impressive on the ground than it had been from the plane. **At one point, I drew their attention to the lush greenery we were passing on the highway. "It's very beautiful," I said to Diana's parents.**

They nodded in agreement. Even though they didn't speak English, they understood the basic sentiment I was trying to express.

After a forty-minute drive, we arrived at what appeared to be a pleasant gated community in an upper-middle-class area of town, where Diana's family had a comfortable three-bedroom apartment on the third floor of a solid brick building. This was common, as I would come to learn, there wasn't a lot of drywall like in North America, everything in Bogota was made of concrete and brick.

Inside, their apartment was cozy and clean; it was a nice change from the hostels I had been staying at during my travels. After giving me an impromptu tour of the apartment, Diana's mother, Marina, began pleasantly fussing over me. She sat me down at the kitchen table and stood over me with care in her eyes and her hands on her hips.

"Are you okay?" she asked in a motherly tone.

I gave her two thumbs up. "I'm okay," I said, smiling.

"Okay," she said.

She gave me a plate of *arepas*, which were cheese filled corn cakes, a popular local dish, and a glass of water to drink. I was more thirsty than hungry, but the food was homemade and delicious, and I ended up finishing it all. Next, they presented me with some small gifts and souvenirs, and a bag of Colombian candies.

Diana's brother Camilo seemed eager to practice his language skills, so I began asking him some general questions about their family. From what I would come to learn, Diana's father had his own video production company, and his wife helped manage the business as well. They also had a few rental apartments, and they were somewhat well off and comfortable by Colombian standards.

The conversation turned to what my plans were while I was in Colombia, and I excitedly told him about the two organizations I was going to work with, a nonprofit called ICBF (Instituto Colombiano de Bienestar Familiar), the Colombian Family Welfare Institute, and Fundacion SION, a small orphanage on the outskirts of Bogota in Suba, run by a husband and wife.

Diana had helped me make all the arrangements, as she was familiar with many of the local orphanages, and several of these places were close to her heart as well. Before she'd moved to Canada, she worked for the Red Cross as a dentist and had given medical care to people in some of the poorest and most violent communities in Colombia, even some in high conflict zones where the government and guerilla factions often waged war. She may be petite, but she was a brave, determined fighter with a big heart.

Camilo asked how I would be getting back and forth to the facilities. "I'll probably take taxis, and when I can, I'll walk as much as possible," I said.

Diana's brother sat up, as if what I'd said alarmed him. He exchanged a few words in Spanish with his parents that I didn't understand, and then he turned back to me. "We'd like to drive you," he said.

Doing his best with a limited English vocabulary, Camilo began giving me some tips for my stay in Bogota and explained that I would need to exercise a little extra caution in my dealings with these organizations, and just in general. Many of the areas of the city were dangerous, and it was better if I didn't wander around, or risk getting lost. **They taught me a local saying, "Don't give papaya," which basically translated as "Don't give bad people the opportunity to take advantage of you."** I got the sense that these people were as cautious as they were caring.

Thanking them all, I took them up on the offer of transportation, and promised I would be extra careful. They seemed satisfied with that.

After our conversation ended, Diana's parents took me to my room, which turned out to be the one Diana had when she was growing up. My heart lifted; I had to smile. There was a tiny bed in the corner, with a pink comforter on it with frilly lace trim. I could imagine her as a little kid, playing with Barbies and hiding under the covers from monsters under the bed. It was perfect. With that, I'd had a long day and the jetlag was starting to catch up with me. I sank down in the soft pink covers, feeling grateful for my accommodations, thankful for Diana's family's warm hospitality, and eager to start my next adventure.

No Place for a 12-Year-Old

***

"No human being is so bad as to be beyond redemption."
—Gandhi

First thing in the morning, Diana's mother drove me to ICBF. Inside the large brick building, I went to the front desk, introduced myself to the staff, and informed them that I had scheduled an appointment with one of their directors, **a man named Christopher who worked in the division that works with child prostitutes.** After waiting a few minutes, one of the staff escorted me to the floor of the institute where Chris's office was located.

The facility immediately reminded me of a university campus, but it was quite dated. You could tell from the furniture; although it was in good working condition, everything looked as if nothing had changed since the 70s. One thing that struck me as we walked through the building, everybody I saw seemed to have a positive energy about them. They weren't bothered or agitated; people seemed to have a purpose.

At the end of a long hallway, I was guided into a large office, and was immediately greeted by a tall slender man with a shock of fluffy white hair and piercing blue eyes. My first thought was that he reminded me of a "nutty professor." He gave me a big smile and welcomed me inside.

"Chris," he said, reaching out and shaking my hand firmly.

"Erik," I said, with a smile.

"Have a seat, Erik," he said, gesturing at two chairs facing his makeshift desk. I lowered myself into a chair, but before I could speak, Chris picked up the phone on his desk —which was ringing loudly— and held his index finger up, silently, indicating for me to wait.

As Chris began speaking a mile a minute in Spanish to whoever was on the other end of the call, I examined my surroundings. His office was sparse, but not sterile, there was a small filing cabinet and messy stacks of papers and files on a small desk. It could have been any office in any first world country, except the walls were solid concrete, with decades old chipped paint. I took a deep breath in; the room had a musty odor that reminded me of an old hospital, with the smell of medicine and faintly rotting lunch, like when the trash needs to be taken out. It was a bit stuffy, and I was restless in my seat, bouncing my leg up and down.

"Sorry," Chris said, setting down the phone with a frown. "So, tell me about the reason you came to Colombia."

I proceeded to tell him that I was on a three-month mission, serving orphaned children and other displaced people. He seemed delighted to hear that and began to share some of his story with me. I was surprised to learn that he was originally a journalist, an expat from Great Britain who had come to Colombia in the 1970s and later ended up working with the programs he'd been reporting on. It was comforting to have a conversation with someone in this program from abroad, someone who had a deep sense of what was happening in Colombia.

Chris started to explain ICBF and its programs to me. While he was talking, a small Nokia flip phone lying face down on his desk started buzzing. He glared at it, growing angrier with each interruption. After it had been ringing nonstop for over a half hour, he suddenly grabbed the out of control device and flipped it over and showed me the screen and worn out buttons.

"This is Lisa's phone," he said, "Look at this, 211 missed calls…and 184 messages in less than two days."

"Unfuckingbelievable!" he said with disgust, then slammed the phone back down on the desk.

"Where is Lisa?" I asked.

"She's taking a shower, then she'll go to see the nurse and doctor and receive treatment for any number of sexually transmitted diseases she surely has."

He continued, "All these calls and messages are from her clients. **It's disgusting the things they're saying to a twelve-year-old.** "Sweetheart," "I miss you," "Baby!" These are all grown men!"

I felt my chest tense up, and heart tighten at the thought.

"Is that common?" I asked.

"Yes and no," he said. "She was passed around quite a bit within the military, so it's common to have this many people looking for her, and her services, so to speak."

He said all this very matter-of-factly. It reminded me how truly naive I was about these types of things. I asked him to tell me more.

"Well, you know in these rural areas, the government puts in the army to protect the towns, and, besides several other factors, such as exploitation, drug addiction, and abuse, some young girls are lured in for the money to survive and because some of the men are looking for paid sex.

"These children, Erik," Chris continued, "live a completely different life than you and me. It's a world most can never explain, understand, or even visualize. Yesterday, there was a mother who was reportedly holding her six-year-old daughter naked on the table while men molested her, and then there's the girl we are talking about today. We try our best to help them when they ask us to, but, over time, you become numb when so many choose to return to the streets."

"Go back to the streets? Why do you think they would go back to that life?" I asked.

"I don't think anyone really knows the reason," he said, rubbing his forehead tiredly. "We just have to do what we do and be there for them when they need us."

I recalled seeing a young dark-haired girl sitting outside of Chris's office, I wondered if she was the Lisa in question. We briefly made eye contact and I saw behind those defiant eyes a tiny flicker of hope for a better life. From what Chris told me, almost 80% of the girls returned to the streets, and at least half of those who did, never saw the age of eighteen. I wondered how soon she'd be back to her life of prostitution, and I feared for her safety.

Chris continued. "When someone like Lisa comes to us, the first thing we do is register her, check for STDs, AIDS, put her through several tests, and get her a place to stay. We try to rehabilitate her and get her off the streets."

"How successful are the programs," I asked?

"Unfortunately, not very successful," he said. "We're facing a lot of challenges."

According to Chris, few of the girls working the streets wanted help because, for some, they were getting their needs met and they were making money for the first time. Chris told me, one of the most successful programs was one where the staff had figured out one way to protect the girls by giving them lubricants. So, when they were penetrated, they didn't get hurt or torn during intercourse; also, some of the men would get excited and ejaculate just before entering them, and, most of the time, it would end right there.

"They feel that's a good way of protecting themselves," he said.

I felt as if I were listening to him speak from far away. My mind was racing with questions, and I flip-flopped between disgust, shock, and futility, until finally I landed on a thought that made sense to me.

"Can I share something with you," I asked, interrupting him.

"Yes, of course," he said.

Leaning forward in my chair, I said, "My core needs are no different than Lisa's. In fact, we're so alike, **I can tell you with complete certainty why she'll go back unless something drastically progresses here.**"

Chris paused, as if taken by surprise. "Okay, go on," he said.

I said, "We all have the same basic needs; it doesn't matter who you are or what you do. We all need to feel we're somebody worthy of this life, which gives us a sense of meaning and significance. In addition, taking in account Maslow's hierarchy of needs, we need to be certain we're going to be okay today and tomorrow. We need challenge and uncertainty, something new and exciting, and we have a deep need for love and connection, to feel warmth and intimacy, that human connection with someone else. Most importantly, we all need to be loved and accepted. These two twin forces shape our lives, and they drive our decisions and make us who we are."

Chris nodded, allowing me to speak without interruption.

I continued. "From what I understand, this 12-year-old girl is, for the most part, is getting her needs met. She's surviving and taking care of herself, she's getting significance by dating these powerful men, she has variety and challenge even though it hurts her, and there's a sense of connection there, not love, but she feels important to these men, as you told me earlier. **There's certainty in this because she knows she can provide her family with food, shelter, and security.**"

Sitting back in my chair, I said, "Now, how are Lisa and I different? We aren't. I just took a different path to meet my needs than she did. We all have the same needs, but we all take different paths, with the resources and beliefs at hand, to have them fulfilled. Only, some people like us believe we have options, but others like Lisa only know and are introduced to a far more disheartening path."

I stood up and looked out the old dirty window of Chris's office. "You see, Chris, why I said I'm just like her? At my core, I too need to be loved and accepted, and I also fear that, at times, I'm not good enough. Unfortunately, most of the time, we don't consider better options or focus on resourcefulness, instead of our limited resources, and find better ways. **The difference is that Lisa doesn't have the tools yet to find better ways of meeting her needs, and possibly doesn't believe that she's worthy of better ways of meeting these needs.**

"But if she discovers new roads and vehicles to fulfill her needs, ones that will give her the same or greater satisfaction than the ones she's currently using, she can leave that life behind. Until then, why would she change the only road she knows to ensure her self-survival? She wouldn't.

Also, if we look at one another as the same heart, the same soul, as true brothers or sisters, then we can go from trying to fix or label someone in need to first seeking to understand."

When we finished talking, Chris stood up to shake my hand. "What you said makes sense," he said. "But trying to implement it and put it into our system... is difficult."

Chris gave me the statistics of how many girls were on the streets and how many boys are being raped and molested in general, it truly was overwhelming. I agreed that the problem was too complex to solve in one sitting. Our conversation ended on a positive note, Chris seemed to understand me intellectually, and I thanked him. We shook hands again at the door, and before I walked away, he warmly encouraged me to come back and discuss it with him again.

After this, I made a point to go back and visit Chris consistently throughout the month as I worked with ICBF. Each time, he always extended an open invitation for me to walk through their various programs and give him feedback. I wasn't a consultant technically; there were far too many layers to this organization serving a country of 43 million people. But I tried to connect with him as much as possible and open up to his perspectives, as he opened up to mine.

After the first week of volunteering at ICBF, one night, Chris called me at Diana's home and asked me to accompany him to visit one of the institutes satellite programs in Bogota, a local foster home. I said yes, as I was excited to see how the outreach portion of the organization touched and served the community in different ways.

A Home in Need of a Heart

✻✻✻

When we arrived at the foster home, I was surprised to see what looked like a house that could have belonged to any family in any neighborhood in Bogota. It was a white stucco building, three stories high, with a little patch of grass in the front yard. Chris gently knocked on the door, with his briefcase in hand, and we stood waiting on the front steps like a couple of salesmen.

After a few minutes, I heard the door unlock, a woman opened the door just a smidge and peered out at us. She seemed to recognize Chris.

"Wait, please," the woman said. "We've had an... incident."

Chris and I looked at each other.

"Of course," he said to her.

Before she closed the door, Chris asked, "What happened?"

They exchanged some words in Spanish —I could tell from Chris's reaction it was something serious— then the woman went back inside, leaving us on the front step. **Chris explained to me that three of the young girls had just tried to kill themselves.** They were between the ages of 6 and 12, two had cut their wrists and the other had broken into the medicine cabinet and swallowed two bottles of pills.

When I heard this, my heart dropped.

Going to this house, I had such high hopes. The place wasn't falling apart, there were no chickens running around the lawn, or broken vehicles out front, everything looked nice and clean on the property, with regular cars parked outside in the driveway. You could almost picture this house in a neighborhood in a suburb of any American city. Yet, something was very wrong inside.

"How often does that happen?" I asked.

He shook his head in silence. His expression answered my question.

For the next ten minutes, we just stood there outside wondering if everything was going to be okay. I kept thinking, *What could lead someone at that age to do that to themselves? What kind of pain are they in that would push them over that limit?* Eventually the door opened again, and the woman let us inside. When we walked in, I was stunned.

I knew from Chris that the organization was very well-defined, with a system of support for the children, and many different resources in place. Some of the children had lived there since they were very young. For others, it was their backup from failed foster care attempts. In this house, they had everything they needed: food, housing, education, counseling, structure –yet something was missing.

To me, the house was cold and lifeless. It wasn't missing love, as the people who worked there clearly cared, but something else even greater seemed to be missing.

Everything was spotless, clean, but there was no heart to it. Maybe it wasn't allowed, or it wasn't a priority. There weren't even any paintings or artwork, just bare white walls with rules posted, how to behave, how to think, how to act. If you had stripped a home of its identity, this is what it would have looked like.

With all the warmth of a company tour, the social worker took us through the house as if nothing had happened. "This is the office," she said, gesturing to a small room on the left side of the building. "Over here is the nurse's area," she said, pointing to a closed door, where I assumed the staff were attending to the three girls. "This is the kitchen, the bedrooms…"

I imagine she was a good and loving person; however, in this moment, she might as well have been saying, "here's our finance department, marketing, and IT instead of bedroom, kitchen, and office.

Unfortunately, it was hard to find anything about this home that could nourish these children's hearts or spirits. Clearly the social workers cared about these young children, but the environment itself was overly clinical and unnerving. It reminded me of a foster care facility that I stayed at for a short time when my mother couldn't take care of us when I was 8 and 9 years old. It wasn't quite as extreme, but it had a similar energy.

When I think back on that time, I remember feeling invisible and unwanted in that place, as if I were a chess piece being moved around on a board. All these people hovering over me, looking at me with clinical sympathy, treating me like I was some broken thing that needed to be fixed, or a problem they had to solve. My mind was literally always racing, and I tried to escape several times before my mother finally came back and got us.

Standing in that foster home was similarly disturbing, and it took me a few moments to shake the bad memories and deja vu it triggered in me. I looked around at the bleak surroundings, and, in that moment, I could imagine why someone, especially a vulnerable young child, might get to a point where they felt hopeless, maybe even invisible, and take them to the verge of despair. It was haunting.

A desire emerged from deep inside me to do something, to make some changes, but I was struggling to find where to start. I thought, *There has to be some way to care for and guide these children, not just physically and intellectually, but also emotionally and spiritually.*

We didn't stay long, and I was secretly relieved. After the tour, Chris and I thanked the staff and got into the car to head back to ICBF. Just as Chris and I were pulling out of the driveway of the foster home, the ambulance came to take the girls to the hospital. I watched the paramedics unloading equipment from the rearview window of the taxi, and I said a little prayer for those three young girls. I heard later that they were able to help them recover, and I knew that the girls would be okay, but the thought of their pain and that moment would stay with me for years.

The Girl with the Broken Arm

***

The month went by so quickly. I was so fascinated with Chris and the work he was doing, and all that I had uncovered in such a short amount of time. That insight I had on the beach in Uruguay about what I needed to do —to heal them— kept building. **In three weeks, I felt I had learned more than I had learned in my entire life.** Every hour, every second, I was learning and unlearning something new.

Thanks to Diana's family, I was somewhere safe and not dealing with a room full of strangers from around the world. Every day, I woke up feeling energized and able to face whatever may come.

One morning the following week, Chris invited me to join him while he worked as a nurse in a local hospital. I marveled at how multitalented he was and always at service to the cause. Diana's mother gave me a ride to the government subsidized hospital, in downtown Bogota, adjacent to the Candelaria area. By the time we arrived, he had already started working so I asked for him at the front desk. Eventually, he came out and brought me to the back where he had a small office.

Chris sat down at his desk and invited me to have a seat in one of the patient chairs facing him. He was wearing blue scrubs, and a white lab coat on top, clipboard in his hand. Although he wasn't a doctor, he spoke fluent Spanish and had the important job of being a conduit between the doctor and the patients. Nurses and support staff were coming in and out of his office while we talked. After about twenty minutes, a young girl was escorted into Chris's office.

She seemed no older than fourteen. **Looking at her, something was familiar about her eyes, and then it occurred to me**— she had that same stare as the boy in Ayacucho, Peru, the boy made of stone, so to speak.

When she spoke, it was short, monotone and very matter-of-fact. She gazed at the wall on the other side of the room, as if her face were frozen in time. She looked like she could care less what happened around her. She would answer questions but wouldn't look either of us in the eyes. I felt that same intense pain inside watching her, not seeing recognition in her, or any spark of spirit, yet I couldn't look away.

She wore a white sling around her neck, her arm was broken.

"What happened?" Chris asked her.

With a blank expression she said, "I was walking across the street and got hit by a car."

Chris turned and looked at me with raised eyebrows, he said, "That's not what happened."

He continued. "Obviously, if she'd gotten hit by a car, she'd have bruises on her legs. I know her mother and grandmother and they're all prostitutes. As soon as they're anywhere from 12 to 16 years of age, they sell themselves. Most likely, her pimp broke her arm in two places."

His words sent shockwaves through my body.

"Why?" I asked.

"Oh, it's usually something minor, but they have to show control. So, he probably broke her arm."

As I was listening to Chris, I was still looking at this child, determined to give her an ounce of life through my eyes, even if it was mine. She was a petite girl, clearly young, but she seemed aged somehow. Old for her years. She was wearing shorts, a warn and fashionably torn t-shirt, and flip flops. If you had seen her on the street in better health, she would have looked like any other teenage girl.

I tried one last time to catch her eyes, but she was so far gone, it appeared as if nothing was there. You could almost imagine her walking in front of a train not caring about anything. It was beyond heart breaking.

After a few minutes, the nurse came to take her away to see the doctor for an X-ray, and I watched her leave the office. There was nothing I could do in that moment. Chris began to explain that it was generational, the mothers in the neighborhood next to the hospital grew up on the streets, and they often didn't go to school. **When they had girls, their daughters became prostitutes, and so on.**

He said, "If the mother doesn't put them into the lifestyle, there is a man around the neighborhood looking to put them in the trade. It's a vicious cycle."

To think about a grandmother selling herself as well, was beyond me.

This was incredibly sad, if true.

I left Chris's office that day feeling as wrong and disgusting as their behavior was, I couldn't label or judge them on just their behavior. If there was even a 1% chance of turning their situation around, I'd rather focus on that, and magnify that opportunity. On the other hand, it wouldn't take much to turn their situation to 100% hopeless, and then they'd be gone forever. There was no way I could get in front of these mothers and find out if there was any hope left, there was too much red tape, and not enough time. Nevertheless, as a witness, just hearing about it was a huge lesson for me about what people will do to meet their needs, but it left me with more questions than answers.

After this, I decided to take a few days off to rest and focus on my physical and mental health, and I invited Diana to come see me. Diana and I had been spending hours on the phone late at night talking, and our separation anxiety was becoming intolerable. We arranged for her to come down and join me for the last week in Bogota while starting my volunteer work at the second organization. Just knowing that I would get to see her soon, filled me with excitement.

With my mental and physical health in mind, I started going to the gym in Bogota called Body Tech, a place Diana's family suggested. Even here, I was also learned a lesson or two.

One afternoon, I was in the gym, running on the treadmill, gazing out of the window facing the street. Below, about two stories down, I noticed what appeared to be a homeless man making rounds along the cars, asking for money. He would wait for the light to change to yellow and drift up to each car window. In Bogota in key areas, there were always several people asking for money at the traffic lights. It wasn't uncommon to see people selling everything from roses to cell phone chargers, even in the nicest neighborhoods with million dollar plus homes. They weren't aggressive, and usually they were friendly, or at least respectful.

Then I noticed something unique about this man, his arm was severely burnt from the top of his hand all the way up to his shoulder, and most intensely on his forearm. **From what I could see, it was still red and raw, and I winced when I caught my first real glimpse of it.** Instinctively, I slowed down on the treadmill, observing his behavior, feeling both curious and concerned. *Someone needs to take him to a hospital and get him cleaned up,* I thought.

I decided to wait a bit and see what happened next. *First, seek to understand.*

The light turned green, and the cars started moving again. My eyes followed the man as he walked into the shade of the trees on the grassy median. Under the trees was a milk jug of water on the ground, and he picked it up and started doing something with it, making vigorous movements. Toweling the sweat off my face, I hopped off the treadmill and went up to the window pane to watch him more closely. I thought, *What is he doing?*

Then I saw it; he was pouring water on his arm, hitting it, making it worse, until it started to bleed.

When the light turned yellow, he set the milk jug down and went back out to show his raw bloody arm to people in their cars, so they could see how bad it was. A woman handed him some change through her rolled down window, and he thanked her. From what I could tell, about half the people would extend their arm out to hand him some money.

That's interesting, I thought.

Immediately I was reminded of the lady I saw in Argentina who slapped her baby to get sympathy from the tourists. Seeing someone self-inflict pain and reinforce their situation to meet their needs in that moment was sobering. Even though there was a solution to his immediate problem right in front of him, he was choosing to keep the problem to meet his needs. I wondered if he fully understood what he was doing.

I'd seen this same scenario now several times in a few different places. I knew there must be some significance. I wondered, *What problems am I keeping? What pain am I inflicting on myself to meet my needs?*

As I finished my workout I had a thought, *It's easier to witness what people are doing and should be doing from the outside, but, sometimes, it also helps to find the answers to our own challenges, why we do some of the things we do to better help someone close to us or the rest of the world.*

SION

*** *** ***

Glancing out the window in Diana's bedroom, I saw the pale blue sky growing lighter outside. The digital clock on the nightstand said 7am. I got out of bed and walked to the kitchen where I saw a small plate of *arepas*, scrambled eggs, and soft cheese, with a mug of steaming hot cocoa next to it. The kitchen was empty; Diana's father had gone to work already, and the housekeeper had left me some breakfast.

Gently sipping on my hot chocolate, I thought about my stay in Colombia so far. I had to admit, it was quite comfortable. By now, Bogota had become one of my favorite places that I'd visited. Despite the many things that were wrong and right about this country, every day, it felt a little more like a potential future home.

By now, I'd had a chance to tour the city and see all its vibrant colors firsthand. In many ways, the city didn't seem like they were going backward. **Despite the corruption in the government, there were still a lot of surprisingly progressive things about Bogota.**

On Sundays in Bogota, they shut down the major avenues, and you could see entire families out on the streets with their kids, walking their dogs, or riding bikes where the traffic would normally be. Bogota was one of the most bicycle friendly cities I'd ever been in, as you could find bike paths all throughout the main arteries of the city. Everywhere I looked, you would see people enjoying the parks and exercising in the outdoor gyms, doing leg lifts and chest presses during the middle of the day. The city had a lot of natural areas, and some areas of Bogota had first-world amenities with trendy restaurants, music venues, museums, shopping centers, and cultural centers, similar to what you'd find in any metropolitan city in North America.

Another thing was the apparent warmth of the people. Wandering around the city, I got lost a few times and was surprised at how easy it was to go up to a police officer and ask directions. I never felt threatened by the police in Colombia. **If you needed help, everybody was there to give you a hand, even if you couldn't speak the language.**

Before my trip to South America, I remember many of my friends and colleagues from around the world asked me, "Why Colombia? Isn't it dangerous?"

It occurred to me that, just like them, most of my preconceived perceptions of Colombia had come from news reports or the movies. As a result, I had a limited view of these countries. It wasn't until I was inside South America, seeing this place for the first time, that I asked myself if these beliefs were based on fears or facts. As I was starting to see, often, the answer was somewhere in between.

I remember seeing a popular ad campaign running for tourism in Colombia at the time, touting that the biggest risk was that "you'll never want to leave."

Maybe they're right, I thought. According to a poll by WIN/ Gallup International Association, Colombia took first place on the "Global Barometer of Hope and Happiness," which surveyed individuals in 54 countries.

A few weeks into my stay in Bogota, and I was already easily starting to imagine what life would be like living there, relaxing on the weekends in the parks, and walking down the wide avenues, shopping, going to local cafes and restaurants. I even wondered if Diana would consider moving back to Bogota. My only personal concern was the food options in Colombia, which back then didn't have the diversity or culinary mastery it commands today and was a bit on the bland side for a home cook like myself. I had to dig hard and deep to find even one Indian or Japanese restaurant in Bogota. Of course, the Colombian staple of beans, rice, and chicken were delicious, but I could see myself growing bored of it pretty fast.

Diana's mother, came into the kitchen and said good morning, pulling me from my daydream.

"Buenos dias, Marina," I said, smiling.

She sat down across from me with a cup of coffee in her hand, and we had breakfast in cozy silence. Besides the language barrier, I had noticed Diana's mother wasn't a very chatty person in general. Diana's father, on the other hand, loved to talk. He was always trying to communicate with me, either directly in Spanish, or translated by his son. I got the sense he was a happy person and generally content with his life; he had a small business and was proud of it.

After we finished our breakfast, Marina and I got into the car and headed to her sister Patricia's house. Diana's aunt would be accompanying us to the

Fundacion SION foster home, the second place I'd arranged to volunteer at in Colombia. Patricia spoke English and would be helping translate for us.

When we arrived at SION, Diana's mother parked the car outside a small house on the outskirts of the northwestern side of Bogota. **Unlike ICBF, Fundacion SION was an independently owned foster home, operated by a husband and wife.** I wasn't sure what to expect after my last experience with Chris at the other foster home.

On the ride there, Diana's mother had mentioned to me that this part of the city was considered a "status 3" neighborhood. There were 6 status levels, I learned. I found it fascinating that Colombia had a tiered system, where utility payments were based on the status of your neighborhood, not your individual income. **At that time, a general construction worker, a maintenance person, or a housekeeper could earn anywhere from $5 a day onward in Colombia.** Someone living in a status 2 area, with very limited access to schools and basic necessities paid much less than someone in a status 6 neighborhood, where only the top 1% of the population back then could afford a well-built and modern home or condo there.

I noticed most dwellings were arranged in one solid block with no separation between the buildings. Each house or apartment boasted its own unique color and accents from the owners, made of concrete, flat and basic, typically with bars on the windows, no grass or yard, and dirt instead of a sidewalk. The neighborhood wasn't overly dirty, but you could tell it was a few levels down from the neighborhood where Diana's parents lived. Looking at the surroundings, I saw power lines overhead and some evidence of a sewage system, so I had to conclude that a status 3 had at the bare minimum, water and electricity. But not much more than that.

We got out of the car and walked up to the front of the home.

As soon as we knocked, a man opened the door; I assumed this was the husband. He introduced himself simply as Jorge, tenderly ushered us inside, and immediately gave us a tour of the modest home. Jorge was quite a bit shorter than me, maybe 5'2" and stout. Once we were inside the main room he turned around, looked up at me with a beautiful smile and gave me a strong warm hug, which I loved, as it felt truly genuine.

The house had three floors, with a polycarbonate corrugated plastic rooftop held up by two by fours. Similar to the place in Peru, an open top floor had laundry facilities and an additional room where a maid would stay if they had one.

During the tour, I got a better sense of Jorge. He seemed generally very proud of what he'd accomplished, but I saw a hint of tiredness around his eyes and in his gestures. Every once in a while, he would give us a little weary smile or a shrug of the shoulders when he was explaining the results of their efforts and their needs. You could tell he was an empathetic individual who was caring for these children with the energy of his heart, and he was doing the best he could. But you could also tell he'd been up against some emotionally heavy challenges and tests.

Halfway through the tour, his wife joined us. She was a little taller than her husband, with a pleasant demeanor, and generally more energy. As we went room to room, I saw some things that were alarming and in need of grave repair. Some of the bunk beds looked like they could fall apart at any moment, and the bathrooms toilets didn't have toilet seats, the kitchen was very basic, and the fridge was half empty. This made me feel quite apprehensive, since there were 28 kids in the house. Judging by the lack of basic amenities in the house, and through my conversations with Jorge and his wife, it was clear they relied solely on donations with no government help.

I need to figure out a way to change that, I thought.

As we continued, the wife opened the door to the kids' rooms to show us where they slept. The children seemed very happy to see me and jumped out of their rooms to come join us for the tour. Inside the small room, I saw that the beds were simple bunks, some had two beds, and some had three stacked on top of each other. I did a little math in my head and realized that there were two children to each small bed, probably sleeping foot to foot. It was less than ideal, for sure.

Unlike any of the other orphanages I visited, this was a very basic, minimalistic DIY type of house. **Even though they housed kids of all ages—some were babies, others were almost 17 years old—still, it felt like a comfortable place to live, and everyone got along.** There were no strict rules or schedules posted on the walls, I imagined whoever got to the bathroom in the morning got to shower first, laundry was done by hand in buckets on the roof, and so on. What impressed me the most was that the founders had two kids of their own. Obviously, they did the best with what they had.

After the tour, Jorge said something in Spanish and excused himself abruptly. I turned to Diana's aunt for a translation.

"He's taking the kids to school now," she said.

When we arrived, I didn't remember seeing a car out front. I wondered how he was going to take them to school. Curious, I followed everyone outside of the house, and saw the husband sitting on an interesting looking bicycle. It was custom made, with built-in racks on the front and back of the frame, with seats big enough for the children to sit on.

With great curiosity, I walked around the bike. Two kids were climbing onto the front seat, and two were already loaded on the back. Jorge could take four kids at a time to school and pick them up the same way after. It had no safety straps or belts that I could see, but still it was safer than walking. I was nervous and quite impressed at the same time.

Even parents in the first world struggled with dropping one or two kids off at school, and here this man was transporting over 20 kids to school every day on a bicycle, pedaling the whole way.

It wasn't even a flat street, there were plenty of potholes, hills, and obstacles to overcome, not to mention they were situated at the bottom of an incline. I stood in front of the house, talking with his wife and children, while watching Jorge go back and forth for the next hour, gently loading the kids onto the bike and ferrying them to school, all without complaint. His shirt was wet with sweat, and he looked exhausted by the time he was finished.

I thought, _This is a dedicated man; no wonder he's exhausted._

That was the first of many things that won me over.

After this, I decided to take a closer look at this organization, to see what I could learn about it. With Diana's aunt translating for us, we sat in the living room and I began my due process, as I had with other organizations, asking the husband and wife some questions about themselves and how they approach caring for the needs of the children. The husband started telling us the story of how he and his wife had started this orphanage.

Diana's aunt turned to me when he was done speaking, and said, "It started out they were just taking care of their own children, but then a woman, a friend of theirs, approached them. She was extremely poor, and not only could she not afford to feed herself or her children but she also was gravely ill and was being admitted to the hospital for several weeks. Out of desperation, she asked Jorge and his wife to take care of her kids while she was away."

Patricia continued. "Once they took those kids in, word got out and a couple more came, and then a couple more next month, and, within a few years, they had over twenty children."

Just as I had suspected, this couple were leading entirely with their hearts. Next, I asked him how long the children had been with them.

The husband told us most of the children had been living in the home for more than a year, but they weren't all abandoned. Some of them had parents in the area, but for one reason or another, they just weren't able to take care of them.

After this, lunch came around, and they served us a very humble meal of seasoned lentils and white rice. After hearing about their struggles with having enough food for the kids, I felt very guilty about eating it. I knew that they had to ration the food carefully, which sometimes meant they could only have one meal per day. **On a good day, they could send the kids to school with a basic lunch and have a small breakfast and dinner, too. But on a bad day, this was all they had.**

Just as with my meal in Chile, never had I appreciated a meal like this, simply because I knew how resourceful they had to be with the scarce supplies they had. I ate my lunch feeling like that meal had been a blessing to receive.

We stayed the entire day at SION, and with each passing minute, I felt something was distinctly unique about this home, but I couldn't quite put my finger on it. This only made me anxious to uncover more. It was the polar opposite of ICBF, where the kids lived in a large, seemingly more organized and sterile institution. Compared to that, these almost thirty children, although they slept end to end in bunk beds and barely had enough to eat, were just normal, smiling, playful, and joyful kids.

Before we left that day, I gave Jorge and his wife a big hug and promised them we would come back the very next day with their permission. Judging by their shining smiles, they looked very pleased to hear that.

The next morning was the date of Diana's arrival from Canada. I got up early, put on my favorite shirt and jeans, and accompanied her whole family to pick her up from the airport. We stood in that sea of people in the terminal entrance, eagerly, scanning the crowd for Diana's face. When

I saw Diana, she was wearing a huge smile, and she bounced up and down in controlled happiness to see our eager faces and hearts. As she turned the corner and exited the crowd of arrivals, she ran over to us, and I grabbed her suitcase while her mother, father and brother hugged her fiercely. Even with her back to me at that moment, she looked even more beautiful than I had remembered.

We spent the rest of the day catching up, hanging around Diana's house. That afternoon, just after an early dinner, Diana and I left for SION. Only this time I invited both Diana's parents to join us, and Diana's father suggested we bring his video equipment along. Being a videographer, he thought it might be nice to do a little filming, with SION's permission, of course. I agreed.

On the way to Suba, I asked Marina to stop at a grocery store so I could buy some food for the children. **Diana and I bought as many groceries as we could fit in the trunk, which took up several large shopping carts.** When we arrived at SION house, we walked in with our arms full of bags of groceries and were greeted by the sight of the grateful faces of the children along with Jorge and his wife. It was a fulfilling and important moment for all of us.

Thankfully, Diana's father captured some of the moments on film, to create a short video to help showcase both the needs and spirits within this beautiful home. Later, we would create a short video to showcase both the needs and spirits within this beautiful home, in hopes that it could be used to get the SION program some additional outside funding.

While we were unloading the groceries and finding interesting ways to make them fit into the century's old tiny fridge, Jorge quickly gathered all the children into the living room. Once they were assembled, the children started to pray out loud for the next hour, going around the room in a circle saying, "thank you God for this house," "thank you for this family," "thank you for Erik coming here," "thank you for this food."

I'd never seen children in these kinds of conditions this intensely grateful and spiritual before. Without understanding all the words, I could feel their immense gratitude and presence of mind, in a very purposeful way. **Some of them stood up and said, "I'm nervous." So they would close their eyes and put their hands on their chest and say their prayers like that.**

Some of these children could easily inspire any priest or preacher, in the way they spoke about God. Just the intensity in their faces spoke volumes, and it was as inspirational as a love-filled church service watching them, if not more. Even when they would trip over their words, or they wanted to say more, but couldn't, I have never felt such love, beauty, and purity from someone's prayer as I did there.

One fourteen-year-old boy stood up and gave what sounded like a sermon, the way he delivered his prayer. Unlike children who've had religion pushed on them, these children weren't just reciting words they thought that grownups wanted them to say; every cell in their body was engaged.

Diana's father continued to respectfully capture the moments, as I sat there in the corner next to Diana listening to their prayers, continuing to be completely blown away. Then, each of them stood up and shared their stories, but not to say, "I'm troubled" or elicit sympathy, they just wanted to talk about who they were and where they'd come from. Because nobody was there telling them they were broken, in that moment, they could just be who they were. And with that, strength poured out of them through their words almost effortlessly.

I thought, *If they're this powerful at this age in their faith and in themselves, imagine what else could be possible for them?*

When they'd finished going around the room, the children turned to me, waiting for me to speak. Because I was so inspired by the moment, first I thanked them for all their beautiful prayers and stories and then I told them a little bit about my story. Then, we all sat on the floor together, and they sang songs about God. I did my best to join them, trying to anticipate the words in Spanish, and from time to time they would stop because everyone was laughing so hard. It was like being part of a big family that wasn't in conflict. For a slight moment, I thought, *For some, this would appear to be some kind of cult.* It was such a new experience for me.

As an organization, SION had the least resources out of all of them, yet they were the most resourceful. And it was all coming from the minds, hearts, and faith inside the children, Jorge, and his wife, not from outside.

We left soon after this, but I was so inspired by my experience there, on the way home I asked Diana's parents if we could go back to the grocery store one more time. It was around 8 or 9 on a Tuesday night, I thought, *Wouldn't it be great to do something really crazy and probably a bit irresponsible? Something fun.*

Inside the brightly lit grocery store, I went to the frozen aisle and bought tubs of chocolate and vanilla ice cream, and sprinkles, and fruit, and fudge, and every outrageous thing I could find to make the craziest ice cream sundaes on the planet.

Diana and her parents were laughing when I got back to the car, my arms filled with bags full of ice cream and toppings. We tossed them in the trunk, and I hopped in the back seat.

"Let's go back," I said with a grin.

It was around 9:30pm when we got back to SION. The lights were still on inside the house. Jorge opened the door. Judging by his expression, he wasn't sure what to make of my surprise visit.

I said, "I know this is irresponsible, and it's late— but have the kids ever had ice cream sundaes before?"

Jorge shook his head in disbelief. "No," he said. I shouldn't have been surprised by his answer, considering some days the children didn't even have enough for lunch or dinner. They relied solely on donations, what they ate entirely depended on the kindness of others. I would soon learn, they didn't even have a freezer.

Pointing at the car, I said, "Well, I have four bags in the car with enough stuff to make the most outrageous ice cream sundaes— chocolate syrup, hot fudge, sprinkles, gummy bears, and bananas. I'd love for you to give it to the kids tonight."

He just looked at me like it was the most amazing and crazy thing he'd ever heard. He had no problem waking the kids, and without hesitation, he called all the children to get out of bed. Then he shouted over his shoulder, "Okay, Erik is going to make you ice cream sundaes!"

Glancing past the doorway, I saw rows of children standing in their pajamas, blinking innocently at him like... *What's that?* Some of them didn't even know what an ice cream sundae was.

This is going to be fun, we all thought.

In the kitchen, the children gathered around the doorway, and solemnly watched as Diana and I started unpacking the bags. At first, they didn't dare get too close, they kept a polite distance, making barely any noise. **Then as we started plating the dessert, some of them started singing, which sparked the beautiful moment further.**

Diana grabbed the ice cream spoon and dug into the soft ice cream. They were amazingly patient, as we scooped ice cream out of the tubs and garnished them with a variety of toppings, not rushing or being greedy. As I started serving them their ice cream sundaes, their eyes lit up. I watched them go giggling off with their plates of ice cream piled high with colorful toppings. It was a beautiful sight.

Was it irresponsible? Yes, probably, but we were all too caught up in the moment.

Childhood memories aren't always supposed to be structured and responsible, they should be spontaneous, and just for the sake of being a kid in the moment. Judging by their smiles and laughter, they loved it. For a second, I was a bit worried they would be too hyper from all the sugar to sleep, but we sang a few more songs, followed by a wave of hugs and prayers again, before retiring back to their beds. As we were packing up to leave, Jorge grasped me firmly by the forearm, and thanked me for giving the children their first ice cream sundae experience.

Diana and I shared a warm glance in the backseat of the car, I grabbed her hand tightly in mine. Seeing her heart and the caring way she interacted with the children had only deepened my love for her. I was starting to unquestioningly see her as my wife, and I was privately continuing to imagine what it would be like spending my life with her.

We went back to Diana's family's home that night, tired, but feeling grateful to have witnessed something so magical, yet so normal, in a home with children who supposedly had nothing.

As I got ready for bed, I saw their smiling faces again and a phrase came to mind, these moments had "pierced my heart."

This was a phrase I remembered from a leadership conference I attended a few years back. We were in a room with about 2,000 people that weekend, and we'd been given an exercise where each of us had to write something profound onto a napkin, and then share it with a stranger in the crowd. I don't remember what I wrote, but the lady next to me turned around and looked me directly in the eyes, then she looked down at her napkin, and handed it to me slowly.

As I took the napkin from her, I thanked her, but kept it closed. We were surrounded by people, turning to each other, exchanging notes, in a sea of chatter, bright lights and blaring music. Waiting for a quiet moment in the chaos, I started to unfold the mysterious message given to me. Opening the uniquely folded napkin, corner by corner, it revealed this timely and pivotal message: "Follow what pierces your heart."

The memory of that phrase stuck with me. For countless years, I always wondered, *what did she mean?*

Now, I finally figured it out. My heart had been pierced. Deep inside me was the desire to let those children know that they were a miracle, and they were already enough. To tell them if they continue to take it one step at a time, instead of focusing on being stuck in their current situation, and if they don't become fooled into thinking that their past is all they are, that they can overcome anything holding them back.

To this day, I still occasionally tell people about the impromptu ice cream sundae party in Colombia. One time, after telling the story to a friend of mine, he gave me a puzzled look, and asked, "Why not spend the money on more groceries rather than ice cream and chocolate sauce?"

Point taken. However, this was the same thinking that permeated the foster house that felt more like an institution than a home.

My conclusion was that we don't always need a reason to give, sometimes we just feel motivated to do what is right for the spirit and joy of others. That night I was motivated by the desire to celebrate the simple things that make childhood fun and memorable, knowing that ultimately our most cherished memories won't be about how much money we had, or the hard times, but about times when we felt loved and shared that love with those around us. **Times when we were given something without any expectation of anything in return, even if it was something as silly as a banana split.**

The last few days of my trip, Diana's parents graciously took us out on several excursions around the countryside to show me the beauty and richness of Colombia. They had been nothing but kind and patient and generous with me, so when they asked me to take some extra suitcases back for Diana, I readily agreed. (Little did I know these extra suitcases would cause me some grief going through customs.) I left Colombia the next morning with a heart full of hope. What started out as a depressing and disheartening visit to Colombia, ended with what turned out to be a deeply heart-piercing experience. Not only was I feeling resolved regarding what I needed to do next, I was riding high on emotion from my time and experience with Diana and her loving family. I left South America, heading back home to Canada filled with plans for the future and a sense of definite purpose.

During the flight, I reflected on all the significant events during my journey. Mainly I thought about the children and insights that had touched my heart and impacted my perception the most. I thought, *I may not be able to protect all of them, but I'm determined to help some of them.* And I was going to start with SION, even if it meant starting my own charitable organization. I couldn't wait to get back to Canada so I could start putting the pieces together to make it all happen.

Part Three
Canada:
What Pierces Your...?

August 2006
Toronto, Canada
✳✳✳

We are all given a gift from God to be a unique light
in this world, a person of value, joy, and inspiration –
who is made from love and made to love. What dictates our
happiness, fulfillment and inner peace is how we nurture,
grow, and share these gifts.
—Erik Kikuchi

The most economical and timely flight I could find out of Colombia had a stopover in Miami, but I was eager to return home as quickly as possible, so I booked it. Sitting on my flight that day, I wondered, after all these intense experiences I had, what it would be like stepping back into a more materialistic and advanced society.

Stepping off the plane in Miami, I was immediately confronted with a chaotic parade of people running, walking, rolling, eating and stretched out every which way as I tried to meander toward my gate. When the opportunity to make eye contact with another person arose, I looked away—and, again, I know this is going to sound strange—because if I didn't, **I would immediately**

seek to look into their eyes to see that person's spirit, essence or gift, if you will. In addition, how they might have looked and behaved as a child. For this reason, I had a hard time looking anyone in the eyes. If I glanced even for more than a second, I would soon get immersed in seeing what made them beautiful from the inside. I also realized that if they shifted their eyes a tiny bit to the left or right, and we locked gazes, they'd probably look back at me like... *What the heck!*

With all this new awareness and heightened sensory acuity I'd accumulated, Miami was a shock to all my senses. In terms of sensory input, it felt like someone had opened up a firehose, full throttle, and pointed it at my head and chest. Walking past store after store filled with what seemed like frivolous and distracting items, I noticed that Miami had a different vibe than South America, and although there was still a strong Latin culture, it had more emphasis and opportunities surrounding materialism (a common growing thread in our first world). After pacing myself, and refocusing on the task at hand, I was able to orient myself and within a few minutes I had navigated through the crowd and hurried to my gate to spend the next few hours waiting for my connecting flight to Toronto.

In the seating area in front of my departure gate I went back into full entrepreneur mode, I had my laptop out on my lap, working on my next project. From time to time, I would glance up to notice the crowd of travelers at the gate. **One older gentleman in particular caught my attention, sitting across from me, about 15 feet away.** He struck me immediately because of his posture and demeanor, how he positioned himself at the edge of his seat. Then I began to notice the hardened lines around his mouth, his eyes, tense and scrunched. He was hunched over, with his back was curled, and his aged arthritic hands cupping his knees. From his overall demeanor, I thought, *He looks quite angry.*

Trying to be as inconspicuous as possible, I took a longer look at the man. I noticed his attire was odd for a man of his age. He wore ARMY style pants with camouflage print, and big thick black ankle-high leather boots with a rugged sole and frayed laces. He had a heavy sweater on, and a money pouch around his waist. *Maybe he's a veteran,* I thought.

Turning back to the computer in my lap, I started making up a story in my mind... *He's alone, he's a veteran, probably going to see his kids and grandchildren. Based on how intense he looks, he probably has a hard time connecting with them.*

As I observed him, I realized of course I was judging him. Because I was only focused on the 1% I could see of this man, I immediately started projecting my own story onto his. At least five minutes in (yes, I stayed present with him that long), I thought, *No wait a minute; I know better than this.*

I decided to try an exercise I'd learned a long time ago called mirroring. The basic concept is that you try to mirror and match another person, to get a better understanding of their internal state, basically what they're thinking and feeling, within a few degrees. In this exercise, you model the other person's physiology, down to their facial expressions and even their breath. If they're tense, you're tense. If their hands are curled, your hands are curled. You match them as much as possible. Though not a science or proven fact, I gave it a try from a distance.

I thought, *This is what I'm going to do.* I put my laptop aside and I sat in my chair, taking short glances at him to get into alignment. I started from my feet up, putting myself into the exact position his body was in. He was leaning approximately 20 degrees forward, back slightly curved, so I leaned forward in my seat 20 degrees, and put my hands on my knees, shoulders slightly up, head down. His lips were curled in a slightly tense snarl, and I noticed he was breathing from his chest, not his stomach. I continued to do this with every part of my body, mirroring his posture, tension, and movements. It took me roughly three minutes to get aligned with him. Once my body was arranged perfectly, I noticed an immediate change. I felt a heaviness in my chest that surprised me—I started to feel sad.

This is fascinating, I thought.

Next, I matched his breathing pattern, and I felt a tightness in my stomach. Without a moment's hesitation, I immediately got up out of my chair and walked over to him. I said, "Sir, is everything okay?"

He looked up at me very slowly, opening his strained eyes as wide as they could go, with a depth of innocence and helplessness. I thought he would have a raspy voice, but he had the softest gentle voice. "Señor," he said in Spanish, "I need to go to the bathroom." Then he paused for what felt like hours to catch his breath. He continued, "And I can't get up." He almost started to cry.

I went nuts. I ran over to the lady at the gate, saying, "We need a wheelchair for this man, and we need to get him to the bathroom." As the attendant wheeled the gentleman off to the washroom, he looked at me and said, "Thank you, thank you," over and over. He was so grateful, my heart fluttered.

I thought back to what the voice had told me on the beach: *heal them.* Maybe I really could make an impact on people if I didn't let the noise of my own thoughts get in the way. This man had gone from what I originally perceived as angry and hardened looking to being the most beautiful person I'd seen in the airport that day. Even more than ever, I realized that it's all about uncovering what lies beyond what we know, or think we know, about a person. We never truly know what's going on, or impacting someone, in each moment we are witnessing. It takes time, compassion, and the will to find the life, the gift, and beauty inside of people, but when you do, it will not only change their lives but yours as well. It's quite remarkable.

Not Even a Thousand Porsches

***

When the immigration officers in Toronto saw my passport with all the stamps in it from the past three months, they pulled me into a private room. I nervously watched as they started popping open my suitcases and going through my luggage one by one. They finally got to the extra suitcases that Diana's parents had given me, and much to my surprise and embarrassment, the officers pulled out several pairs of women's underwear. The officers asked me a lot of questions, but despite their suspicions (and raised eyebrows), they seemed satisfied with my answers, and eventually let me go through customs.

As I left the Toronto airport, I grabbed a cab outside, both grateful and elated to get back to my familiar life. I was pleasantly anticipating walking around my favorite parts of town, seeing old friends, and taking comfort in my daily routine. **Knowing without a doubt that material items don't ultimately make us happy, I was still overly excited to drive my sports car.** I'd been taking taxis and buses and walking for the past three months, and I was looking forward to my Porsche. In fact, in that moment, being in control behind the wheel of such a powerful machine was all I could think about.

The first thing I did was go directly back to my old office to meet my ex-wife Andrea so I could see how she had been doing the past few months and retrieve the keys from her. Our separation was amicable, and I'd entrusted her with my Porsche while I was gone, so she could take care of it and enjoy it. When I arrived, I set my things down in front of the entrance, said hello to the team, and went straight into my old office. Andrea walked in just as I was filling some paperwork I needed to take care of. She greeted me with a smile, but something in her demeanor was standoffish.

After a few minutes of chatting, I could tell she wasn't that interested in hearing about my trip, and she had better things to do.

"Thank you for taking care of the car," I said.

Short and to the point, she put the keys on the edge of the desk. "I didn't drive it much," she said.

Scooping the keys off the desk, I thanked her again, lowered my head, and quietly left the office. Outside, I took the stairs two at a time, like a school boy on his way to play with an old friend. I spotted the back bumper of my beloved car in the parking garage and stood back for a moment admiring her (why do we call a car her?). It was like seeing my car again for the first time. **I was so filled up emotionally from my trip, this was just the icing on the cake.**

Eagerly climbing into the driver's seat, I sank down in that perfectly comfortable contoured leather with a sigh. Owning a Porsche, for a boy who grew up sleeping in parks and never went to college, was still a pillar of accomplishment for me. Feeling the familiar weight of the keys in the palm of my hand, I put the key in the ignition and heard that vroom. I hit the button to lower the top down and pulled out of the garage just as my favorite song (Feel Good Inc. by the Gorillaz) was playing on the radio. What an awesome feeling.

My office was right next to a major train station, just outside of Brampton. It wasn't an area where you could drive a Porsche, but there were a few alleyways where I knew I could have some fun. I peeled out of the driveway and made a sharp left, anticipating the familiar rush and exhilaration of driving. But something was wrong—I felt empty.

What's going on, I thought? I rolled up to the stop sign and sat there dumbfounded.

The excitement, the thrill, and the happiness I used to feel from driving my pride and joy—at that very moment was nonexistent. My mind was scrambling. It was as if none of what I had accomplished in the last 8 years of building my business or achieving wealth mattered. **The weight of that feeling pulled the bottom of my heart, and I felt my mind slowly sinking to a dark place without answers.**

I shook the feeling off. Maybe I just needed to try again.

Up ahead, I saw a little back alleyway where I could go around a corner at a higher speed. I hit the gas pedal and the car accelerated with the rumble of exhaust bouncing off the trees and buildings, and ever-increasing speed. Again, I took the corner with power and control, with a bit of a no-holds-barred kick this time. As I slipped out the back in a controlled drift, I waited for that familiar surge of adrenaline, but it never came. A voice in my head screamed, *No. NO. Something is wrong.*

After making the turn, I realized the feeling wasn't simply going to turn on, and I needed to do something about it. I literally stopped at the next stop sign, pulled over, and put my hazards on.

Turning the engine off, I sat there with my arms crossed like a spoiled kid, staring blankly at the Porsche emblem on the steering wheel. It could have been a cheese sandwich that I was staring at instead of a Porsche symbol, for all I cared. My interpretation, and the feeling would have been the same.

I was genuinely confused. For the last ten years, I had always fought for what I thought I always wanted. My goal back then was to have my own company, hit over a million dollars in sales, and I would like to own a Porsche all by the age of 31. And I had gotten everything I'd ever wished for.

Now I was sitting there in full realization that this Porsche wasn't a key to happiness. This sounds intellectually correct, and you're probably thinking—*of course!* But for me, it wasn't so obvious.

For others, happiness could be found in buying their first house, or advancement in their career, or anything they've invested time, intention, and focus to feel a sense of identity, accomplishment, and/or security. It doesn't have to be a car. Anything that we chase to fuel self-worth that's temporary is just that—temporary.

This wasn't an intellectual epiphany I was having. I was feeling this from the inside out, as I was both being present with myself and honest about how empty this situation was. Incredulously, I thought, *How could I be chasing something so shallow for so long, thinking success in wealth and material things was the only source of happiness in my life?*

It may sound crazy, or as if I'm overexaggerating, but this wasn't some irrational response. In that moment, after spending the last three months serving and working in South America and thinking back over the eight years I spent building my first company, it finally hit me that what I was chasing this whole time wasn't real happiness. It was temporary happiness.

Driving my Porsche couldn't compare to the feeling of true happiness I had experienced in my travels across South America. Those moments sitting with the children on the couch, being truly present while they talked and played, being their unique selves. Moments of listening to them without judgment, playing without having to prove anything, and appreciating them as they were right in that moment. **That feeling of contributing to someone, truly connecting, or seeing someone's gift within them—nothing that I could have accomplished or attained materially compared to that.** Not a Porsche, not even a thousand Porsches!

Something inside me surrendered, I was no longer concerned with trying to get a quick thrill from driving that day. I drove home mindful of my surroundings, with a sense of curiosity, and peace at the same time, thinking, *All this time I've been chasing the wrong thing!*

Diana

✳✳✳

When I arrived home that evening, the first thing I noticed was how quiet it was. The sidewalks were so empty, as I drove through my neighborhood, it felt as if everyone had left the city. I had spent the past three months surrounded by so much activity and life, and had experienced so much heart, conflict, and emotion, and had grown accustomed to this symphony. Even though I was happy to be back home, it was a bit anticlimactic.

After my house in Caledon sold, I purchased a main residence in Kitchener, Ontario, and rented the basement apartment to a subletter, Adrian, while I was away. The basement light was on, so I knew Adrian was home that evening. *At least there's someone home,* I thought.

As I entered the house, Adrian came up from below and around to the front door to say hello. After chatting for a few minutes with him, I put my bags in my bedroom and jumped in the shower. I had plans to pick up Diana that evening and take her to dinner; I couldn't wait to see her.

When I arrived at Diana's place, she came out dressed beautifully as usual. I got out of the car and went around to open the door for her, and she slid into the front seat and gave me a hug and a kiss. **Right away, I noticed a slight disconnect between us, but I couldn't quite put my finger on it.** Maybe because we'd built up this image of our relationship and amplified our feelings so much over the past three months. The love was still there between us, but the fantasy couldn't quite live up to the reality.

As we drove to the restaurant and made small talk (it felt more like silence to me), I looked out the window and noticed how drab and gray the city looked. It all seemed so lifeless compared to the lively markets and city streets of Argentina, Chile, or Colombia. Then, I said something really stupid.

"This is really boring," I said to break the silence.

What I had meant to say was "this environment is boring" but instead the laziest brain cell in my head had spoken. In my mind, I was trying to say that there wasn't enough life here, everything felt neutral. But looking back now, I'm sure Diana interpreted that as me saying *she* was boring. In that moment, I didn't realize what a big blunder I'd made. **Diana was a quiet lady, but, of course, with a statement like that, she grew even more quiet than usual.** We drove to the restaurant in complete silence, which was strange for us. We'd spent the last three months declaring our affection for each other and sending hundreds of emails back and forth, but now, I couldn't think of anything to say to her. For some reason, I was at a loss for words.

That night, we went to a Thai restaurant, and that place was boring, too. It wasn't empty; plenty of tables were full of people dining quietly, but the atmosphere had this "lifeless" feeling to it. In South America, people seemed to be more in their essence, free to be expressive and emotive, but in North America, people were much more restrained. As we sat at our table, I made another unfortunate off-hand comment to Diana, and it was a bit of a downslope from there. This time, I realized I'd said something wrong, and I quickly tried to explain it to Diana, but, unfortunately, the damage was done.

The rest of the night was tense, with an ever-deepening silence. By the time I dropped her off, things had gotten even more quiet between us. When we pulled up to her apartment, Diana politely said goodnight, and got out of the car. I went home alone.

This rejection triggered a chain reaction of confusing thoughts and emotions for me (and I'm sure Diana as well). I felt like a foreigner in my own environment, as if I had spent the last three months in a place full of life, diversity, and vibrant colors, and now I came back to a world of black and white. I came to realize it wasn't my actual environment I was perceiving, but a feeling from the inside, that caused me to see it through an entirely new lens. Because the gap between the two experiences was so wide, I was sitting in my house thinking, *what do I do now?*

I knew I had to start attending to my business, but I was disoriented. I could build a business, but for what? I thought, *I'm not contributing anything meaningful for anyone else right now.* It felt empty, and I knew buying things wasn't going to help.

Unable to answer that question, I decided to try and meet up with some friends, hoping maybe I would get some inspiration for my next business plan by talking to other people in my personal network. I received an invitation from some friends to attend a birthday party a few nights later, and I decided to meet up with them.

After a half hour at the party, I found myself standing around talking with my best friend and a few other guys. The conversation revolved around cars, as some of them had seen me drive up in my Porsche and they started asking me details such as HP, torque, year, etc. I found the topic quite boring, but I didn't want to be rude, so I answered their questions, while sipping my drink, hoping someone else might call me away. Next, the topic of discussion moved to renovating their houses and other things they had bought, will buy, or were hoping to buy, and then they began talking about work and money. **With every passing second, I felt like I was dying inside.**

I thought, *There's so much more to life than talking about our things and money!* I wanted to talk about things that really mattered. I wanted to connect with my friends, and ask what inspires them? What fuels their heart? What keeps them up at night? But there was no way I could ask anyone a serious question, without it seeming hopelessly out of context.

The conversation was so surface level, it disturbed me - because I was that person for such a long time. Eventually I stopped talking altogether, and just stood there awkwardly listening to them speak about their stocks and their homes and their luxury sports cars. **They could probably tell something was different about me, and my feeling of isolation grew.** For the first time in months, I felt uncomfortable in my own familiar environment, not because I couldn't contribute to the conversation, but because I felt at the time, I didn't have anyone to relate to.

If my only option was to have a conversation about stuff that didn't really matter, then I'd rather be at home focusing on other things. Looking for an opportune moment to slip away unnoticed, I left the party that night feeling even more disoriented than I had before I'd arrived.

After that night, I threw myself into my responsibilities. Getting back to working on my next business, a localization and packaging company for the videogame industry. I began expanding it in earnest. This time, I was building the company and the team to be completely remote, so I wasn't tied to one place. As I hired my team, I drew from talent all across the two continents, Canada, Brazil, and Mexico, so I could feasibly work from anywhere in the world. An exciting thought occurred to me, *Maybe I could even return to South America someday soon.*

Punks on a Rock

***

A few days after I had been in Canada, I was heading to a business meeting around lunchtime in my car. I was very thirsty, and I wanted to be hydrated for the meeting, so I ran into variety store about five blocks from my house to get some water.

As I got out of my car, I saw two teenagers sitting on a rock about fifteen feet away, in the little patch of green between the street and the parking lot. They were a young boy and girl sitting side by side, who looked to be about

15 or 16 years old. They were dressed in punk rock gear, dog collars around their necks, ripped t-shirts and beat up black leather jackets. The guy had his head shaved on one side, and the young lady had on thick black boots and a plaid skirt.

They stood out to me right away because I used to dress like a punk rocker when I was in high school. The sight of them made me immediately smile and think about a time when I wasn't so confined about what I thought I should or shouldn't do to fit in. As I got back into my car and took a better look at them, I thought, with a little bit of envy, *I wish I were them right now.*

Exiting the parking lot, I passed right by them. A thought occurred to me, and I wondered if they got judged for how they looked by their friends and families, the way I did. About halfway down the road, I was inspired, feeling suddenly free from being confined, and I made a U-turn, and decided to go back.

I wasn't sure what I was going to say to them exactly, but I remembered exactly where they were sitting, and I pulled up right beside them. I was wearing my nicest Armani suit that day and driving my Porsche, so I must have looked pretty conspicuous. **They kind of looked at me, not aggressive, but puzzled,** like *What's this guy doing?*

I said, "Hey listen, I don't normally do this, and it's not about me, but I wanted to share that when I was your age, I dressed exactly like you. I struggled in school, and I definitely didn't fit into the norms. I was judged a lot by how I looked, and that closed several doors for me back then as well. I don't know if this is your reality, but if so, I just wanted you to know that moving forward there's hope for us who have everything against us, especially if we don't fit the norm."

Then they looked at each other, both a bit in shock, and yelled out "That's so cool! Thanks man!"

Immediately after that, I drove off. I didn't know what their story was, or their exact situation, but most people would see them as underdogs, and I wanted to honor that 1% they were showing to the world, while also acknowledging the value and potential that was underneath it. Their smiles made my day. It erased all the shallow, disconnected conversations and experiences I'd been having with people since I'd been back. This single interaction, connecting with these two human beings, gave me the fuel I needed to shift my focus back onto my real passion: making a difference.

It wasn't long before my business started to take off and we made headway and contracts with some of the bigger players in the video game industry; such as Activision, Sega, and Sony. With a few successful contracts under my belt, I felt comfortable enough to shift my focus back onto my philanthropic pursuits, and the people I met in Colombia. Ever since I found SION, it seemed to become the center of the universe for me. At first, I had been attracted to it because of their energy, hope, and need, and now, I was certain God had brought me there for a purpose.

My first inclination was to help them repair the house; it was in such a state of disrepair, the plumbing was a mess, they didn't have gas to cook their food with, and the beds were starting to fall apart. Solving these problems would have made an immediate improvement in their living standards regarding their health and safety. Despite the lack of infrastructure, the faith and sense of community this family had was incredible. I wondered, *If they had these extra tools, how much further could they go?*

The house became a driving force for me. I spent the next few months, flying back and forth from Toronto to Fundacion SION, working with a small team, documenting the things they needed so I could get estimates for repairs on the bathrooms, bedrooms, and the kitchen. As I went through the estimates, I began asking myself a different set of questions. I thought, *What if Jorge couldn't bike them to school that day because he was sick? What if I found them a much bigger home in a neighborhood closer to the bus lines? And if I did find them a house, how would I pay for it?*

My mind started playing with the idea of buying them a new, safer and larger home. *Okay, but how?*

By this time, I had spent a lot of money traveling back and forth, and I knew from experience that throwing or investing money at things doesn't always immediately solve problems. My intention wasn't to spend my life savings here, but to make a significant difference in these children's lives. Rather than coming up with reasons why I should or shouldn't continue doing this, I decided to follow through on my dream of buying a bigger house for SION. I didn't have the money to do it myself, I wasn't liquid enough, so I decided I would have to ask my network for support.

Slowly, I began sharing my story with some of my more affluent friends. I wrote a description of my experience working with SION and sent some videos to a few key people. I wasn't giving anyone a hard sell, just putting feelers out. People kept saying things like, "I'd love to help, but things are tight," or "I wish I could do more to help you." I hadn't given up hope at this point, but around the fifth month, I thought, *It's not going to happen.*

After seven months of pushing through, a miracle happened. I remember the moment vividly: getting out of my car on a rainy day, heading to the gym around 2pm, and hearing my phone ring. My friend Rod's name flashed on the screen of my phone. Rod was someone I met ten years prior, and he was one of my more affluent friends. He owned hundreds of rental properties in Florida and other parts of the U.S., and I considered him both very intelligent and a very successful self-made man. I was at the front door of the gym when I answered the call.

"Hello?" I said.

"Erik, hi, I got the CD and the letter you sent about SION and I'd like to help fund your project."

"What do you mean?"

"I'd like to buy the house," Rod said.

My eyes stung with tears. I stood there for a moment, in total shock.

I said, "You mean the down payment?

"No," he said. "The whole house."

He continued without hesitation. "You go find the house and I'll give you what you need. Let's talk more later this week, I just wanted to tell you this, so you can start moving."

After I hung up the phone with Rod, my heart continued to soar. My mind went into gear immediately, thinking of all the things I would need to make this dream happen. I imagined how excited Jorge and his wife would be to hear the good news. Not one week later, I was back in Colombia.

A Home for SION

***

This time, my trip to Colombia was much different; it was mostly business. Diana and I had broken up, so I had to plan my entire trip and get around on my own. This added an extra layer of responsibilities to my trip, but I was so determined and focused on the task at hand, it wasn't a concern. I immediately set about studying the housing market in Bogota, looking for a translator, and found several surprising things.

Back then, if you were interested in buying a house in Bogota, you couldn't just go to a Coldwell Banker or ReMax. They had those there, but most of the home sales were made through the home owners themselves.

You had to drive through neighborhoods, and see for yourself, and I also discovered there was no set standard of prices. Whatever someone thought the house was worth was its price. And the prices were all over the map.

The day after I arrived in Bogota, I went out looking for houses. I started early in the morning. I decided the best way to go about this would be to hire a cab. The taxi came and picked me up at the hotel, and I climbed into the backseat armed with my Spanish-English dictionary and a preplanned set of phrases to help him understand where to take me. By this time, I knew a little more Spanish, and I felt confident I could get my intentions across. To my surprise, when I told him where I was going, the taxi driver answered me in English!

I'm in luck, I thought.

My driver seemed eager to talk, and he chatted with me freely, glancing back at me from the rearview mirror as he was driving. He told me his name was Carlos.

"Where are you from?" Carlos asked me.

"Canada," I said.

To my astonishment, he began speaking French to me! He was so proud of his language skills, and I was thoroughly impressed, even though I don't even speak French.

I really liked this guy. I thought, *This is someone I could use to help me look for houses.*

Without telling him too many details, I asked him if I could hire him every day to go look around the different neighborhoods to search for a property. He gladly accepted the offer. Of course, at the time, I didn't realize how things worked. I would soon find out he was negotiating a commission with the home owners, and if I bought a house through his referral, it could be as high as 20% or more. Good or bad, I didn't know it at the time, and I was just really focused on my first priority, finding a home.

The next day, Carlos picked me up and we spent the afternoon touring the neighborhoods, while I was communicating back and forth with Jorge to work out the logistics. I was there for three weeks, and by the time I was done, I had accumulated data on over 50 houses all around Bogota and the surrounding cities. Meanwhile, I visited Jorge and his wife at SION quite frequently to give them little updates on the progress of the house hunting.

Fortunately, Diana's family was still on good terms with me, and her father went back to SION with me a few times, and we did some more filming while I was updating them. What I learned was that most Colombians, not just Diana's family, are passionate about the needs of others. In all my travels in that country, I didn't meet a single person who wasn't doing something for someone. **This wasn't like my personal experience in Canada, where we're typically too busy and tend to allow others with more time and resources to help the less fortunate.** It was bigger than that for most Colombians I came across; it was almost part of their national identity.

Over the next few months, I went back to Colombia two or three times, and each trip I would send reports back to Rod. It was taking longer than I had anticipated because I didn't want just any house, I wanted it to be sustainable, and in a good location for schools. I owned rental properties, so I knew what I was looking for. Rod was patient, and I appreciated that.

During one of my extended stays in Bogota, I decided to call my friend Chris from ICBF and invite him to have coffee with me. I was eager to tell him about the SION house and get his opinion on what I was doing. **The project seemed to pique his curiosity, and he immediately started asking me a lot of questions.**

"This is very interesting; do they have access to medical care?" he asked.

I told him I wasn't sure, but I highly doubted it.

Chris continued, "It's important for them to get checked, especially if they've been abused; they could have any number of issues or diseases."

He said this with the authority of a doctor, and I let him know I respected his professional opinion and agreed with him. "How can we have that testing done?" I asked.

"There's a place you can send all the children and they can get checked for STDs and find appropriate treatments without cost," he said, and he wrote down the name of a clinic on the napkin and gave it to me.

Later, when I talked with Jorge and his wife about it, they seemed surprisingly uneasy. Jorge's wife especially seemed skeptical and proceeded to ask a lot of questions such as "who is this person" and "what are they going to do?" I reassured her by letting her know that Chris was a close friend, and I tried to encourage them, urging them that this was important, as I knew that a few of the boys in the house had been consistently abused and raped. Eventually, Jorge and his wife agreed to let the kids get tested.

We had it all organized; the next morning, I went to the house early to pick up the kids. Jorge only sent a handful of the children with me, and I got them into the three taxis without much hassle. When we arrived at the building where the clinic was, Chris ushered us into the waiting room and started taking the children in the back to check them one by one, while the nurses ran blood and urine tests.

The testing took much longer than I expected, and we wound up being there all morning. I sat patiently in the waiting room. I was just a conduit for this opportunity for the children; I wasn't directly involved with the cases. **Everything was strictly confidential, and I was sure that Chris wouldn't have shared their medical status with me even if I had asked.** When all the check-ups were done, I thanked Chris, and took the kids back to the house.

The rest of the trip I went back and revisited a handful of houses that would make a great home for the children, before flying back home to Canada feeling very satisfied. By the time I left, I had some strong leads on a few very nice houses within our price range, and I felt things were going according to plan. There seemed to be no reason to worry about the project at all. One night, a couple of weeks after I had left, Jorge called me crying, "What did you do?" he said, over and over.

He was so distraught, the language barrier was too much, and I couldn't figure out what was going on. In a panic, I booked a flight down to Colombia.

By the time I arrived, Jorge wasn't returning any of my calls, and I had to do some digging. I asked some friends to call him and see what was going on, and while I was waiting for them to get back to me, I decided to call Chris.

Then I learned what happened.

After the kids had been tested, ICBF had found out where the children were living and inspected the SION house. They had deemed it unfit for the wellbeing of the children. Chris informed me that the children shouldn't be sleeping two to each bed, and the house was unhygienic. Not dirty, but not up to clinical standards. They had brought two buses and removed half the children from the home so it could just hold the right number of children per bed. The SION house was still there, but it would never be the same.

With a heavy heart, I asked him where the children were placed. He told me they'd put the children in various homes for children around Bogota. My only thought was that these kids living in homes like the one where the girls had tried to kill themselves. As he told me all this, I felt a searing pain in my chest. It tore me apart.

When I got off the phone with Chris, I sat down on the edge of the bed in the hotel room and put my head in my hands and cried. I felt like I was taking more steps back then ahead, I wasn't sure what the next step was.

At the same time, I still wanted to get that house for them so Jorge and his wife could get the kids back. I had a glimmer of hope left that perhaps I could make this situation alright in the end. But first I would have to be completely transparent with our donor. From that very hotel room, I called Rod right away and told him what had happened. I'm sure he could hear the anger and frustration in my voice. It had been four months, but I need more time.

He said softly, "I'm sorry, Erik, I wish I could help, but a lot of time has passed, and I meant to call you, but I've found another place for the money."

My heart sank to a level I'd never imagined possible. Thinking about how I'd let down Jorge, the children, Rod... everything I did during that whole trip, in that moment I felt, *What was it all for?* It made me so angry. I had spent a considerable amount of time and heart just going back and forth to Colombia the past few months and it all ended up shutting down in my face. Regrettably, it all ended there—helping the children to get back together, finding the house to keep them together, building the programs to help them grow and not repeat their past with their own children—all of it.

It took me many years to process what had happened with the SION house. I made attempts to find the children who had been dispersed into the foster system but was largely unsuccessful. I finally got in touch with Jorge and made amends as best I could, and some of the children there that had touched my heart. This provided me with some solace. Over the coming months, **I continued to put energy into creating a charitable foundation, but it became a struggle as personal finances began to diminish.** Eventually, I decided to end my pursuit with building the foundation, holding onto the belief that God's delays aren't always God's denials.

Sometimes, when I tell this story to people, I get an understandably contrasting reaction. They want to know why I was helping people in Colombia when there were so many people at home to help.

One can definitely make an argument for helping those at home versus those in other countries. With this, I always tried to keep my answers heartfelt and simple. First, I tell them I had a calling for these children, one that pulled me to take action despite my own excuses of why I couldn't or shouldn't. Secondly, I know all of us are here for a reason, and my reason back then was to find out what impoverished and abandoned children needed to have a better quality of life. Thirdly, we're all brothers and sisters, regardless if we live next door or thousands of miles away.

With this, I would close with, "Follow where your heart is pierced, and do what's necessary."

As of the writing of this book, I've had the opportunity to work, serve, and visit over 45 countries and 160 cities around the world. Before I started this journey in South America I was literally obsessed with work and growing my business. My mind was consumed with money, business, and achieving an abundant lifestyle, because I believed my self-worth was a direct reflection of these things. More money meant success, and more success meant that I was becoming "somebody" important. Spending time with anyone back then without a specific agenda or purpose was simply out of the question, and any unexpected conversation eventually headed toward business or opportunities.

Little did I know, in my pursuit of success, that fear was writing most of the story in my mind and pulling me further me into the dark abyss of temporary happiness. Embarrassingly, I didn't realize that my fear was disguised as drive. Fear of not being enough, fear of not deserving love, fear of failure.

During my travels, I've noticed how easy it is to see others through eyes that are clouded with projections and prejudgments of what we think we know or what we believe something should be. As a result, we all, too often, end up judging others, categorizing them, or simply being unkind or disconnected to one another out of ignorance. **I've also come to see firsthand,**

that no matter the location, person, or circumstances, love connects us all, while fear separates us.

Cultivating this type of love begins by clearing away our "blinders" and truly seeing, appreciating, and believing in each other as imperfect, uniquely gifted individuals who all want to be someone worthy of love. If we can see this first, we can continue to foster that feeling in each other without fear, even in life's most difficult moments. I'm living proof that you can go beyond the routine of what we know, where we feel temporarily safe and happy, and find something much bigger and more fulfilling. And you don't even have to travel far to practice this, you can start right now, even right where you're sitting.

So, what pierces your heart? Because, at the end of the day, of course, our accomplishments matter, but ultimately, we have to ask ourselves with both love and patience, *Who is it all for?*

"Start by doing what's necessary; then do what's possible; and suddenly you are doing the impossible."
—St. Francis of Assisi

Epilogue:
Together For
The Greater Good

April 2019
Bogotá, Colombia
***

S tanding in front of the restaurant, I glanced down at my phone to check the time. Out of the corner of my eye, I saw a young woman standing across the street. She waved and walked anxiously up to me. I recognized her immediately and my heart filled as I saw the little boy holding tightly onto her hand.

It had been more than ten years since I last saw any of the children from SION house, so it was surprising, a few months ago, when I received an email from Lizzy, one of the girls who had stayed behind after half of the kids were removed from the home. After exchanging a few emails back and forth with Lizzy, I took the opportunity to invite her to lunch, as I was returning to Colombia to visit family with my wife Johana (who was from Colombia as well) and my daughter Elizabeth.

As we waited outside for my wife and daughter to arrive, I took a moment to observe the young woman standing in front of me. The last time I saw her she was an 11-year-old girl with a wonderfully darling overbite and thick glasses, wearing mismatched hand-me-downs, and now she was a cordial well-dressed young lady in her twenties. Not only was she a mother herself with a 7-year-old son by her side, she was expecting her second child in a few months. There was no sign of the shy awkward teenager I'd met in 2006. **I was happy for her about how poised and mature she presented herself, and I told her as much.** She smiled and thanked me, with an air of modest self-confidence, as she leaned over and kissed her son on his forehead.

Just then, my wife and daughter pulled up in a taxi. They waved eagerly to us as they paid the fare and collected their things. Once we all gathered on the side of the street, Johana hugged Lizzy with open arms. The gratitude and smiles on their faces lit the entire scene. With that, they immediately began speaking in Spanish and didn't stop, which seemed like the entire time. After we finished our greetings, we walked across the street to our reservation at a simple but elegant bistro in the trendier neighborhood of Usaquén. I had booked this place to show Lizzy my appreciation, and it was also in a neighborhood I used to frequent often while living there.

As we approached the door, Lizzy slowed her pace down momentarily. I sensed she was intimidated to go inside what appeared to be an upscale restaurant. Even though she and her husband were able to pay rent, had a decent place to live, and she worked as a nurse, she was still considered lower class. Acknowledging her concern, I wanted her to know she was just as worthy of being there as anyone, if not more, as she had probably overcome far more than most people sitting in there. I reached for the door, bowed slightly, and motioned for her and her son to enter first.

Once inside, Lizzy looked around the restaurant, smiled, and looked over to quietly share with me, "Erik, this is the first time I've been in a place where people have napkins in their lap." I smiled and joked with her that they do it for good manners, but it's also a clever way to hide nasty food. She laughed.

After we were seated and ordered lunch, Lizzy and I began to talk more. She seemed eager to share with me the story of her life after I left. Her son was extremely well behaved, and I marveled at how quietly he sat through the entire meal. My daughter Elizabeth sat next to him and they handed the dishes back and forth, sharing the meal and attentively listening to Lizzy. As she spoke, I remembered my time with her when she was in SION house, sitting on the couch with her listening to her talk about how her mother had to give her and her sister up. Even back then, I sensed that she was very secure in her faith, and she knew her life would only improve.

She talked about her struggles with school. "I was starting to fail in my classes," Lizzy said. "I had trouble focusing in class because I couldn't see the blackboard, and I would constantly suffer headaches. Do you remember buying me glasses?"

On one of my trips to SION, I ended up taking her and three other girls to get their eyes checked and discovered that the donated glasses they were wearing were the wrong prescription! It was a small thing, but I ordered the girls some new glasses with their correct prescriptions.

"Yes, I remember," I said.

Lizzy continued. "After I got those new glasses, everything turned around for me. That's why I became a nurse. If I had continued wearing the wrong prescription I wouldn't have continued going to school, and I could have ended up in a completely different life than I have today."

When she told me this, my wife put her hand lovingly on my leg, and I bowed my head and smiled. I was genuinely moved to hear this; I never thought that something as small as glasses could change someone's life. Here I was overthinking it this whole time, always wondering, *Did I do enough for these children? Was it too little? I never got them the new house I had promised...*

This young girl took something as simple and necessary as her eyesight and used it to grow and flourish. Of course, it wasn't just the glasses, Lizzy had something inside her that allowed her to take that opportunity and make something of it. In fact, I could sense this strength she had when I first met her. She was one of the children with whom I had shared a little bit about my story and encouraged her to use the past as a reason to move forward. I told her to be courageous and to always find ways to make the best out of whatever she faced in life.

Reflecting back on my experiences in South America in 2006, I didn't believe in God at the time, but I believed in a spirit or something greater than ourselves. The strength of these children wasn't completely lost on me, but it had taken the greater part of ten years to realize how the power of faith can fill someone from the inside out. Those with faith aren't so reliant on temporary, external needs, and Lizzy was the living proof of this.

With a deep sense of gratitude in her voice, Lizzy began thanking me for our time together so many years ago. She thanked me for being patient with her, even though I didn't understand her at the time. "You made me feel as if I was somebody; at the same time, I had a sense of inspiration. I thought if you went through similar things, even in a different country, I felt empowered and worthy enough to do something more with my life."

By the end of our meal, my feeling of pride for Lizzy had grown enormously. **The fact that Lizzy had gone on to have a family and a career was proof that those of us who've been considered "disadvantaged" can still rise above our past and make our lives an inspiration to others, not a warning.** Unfortunately, not all the children in SION house grew into positive role models as Lizzy did, a small minority of the kids joined gangs and some of them are still struggling, but for them, faith remains.

I'd also come to the conclusion that it doesn't matter whether we make grandiose gestures or small ripples of service throughout our day, week, or lifetime. Giving doesn't have a minimum or maximum requirement. We should do what we can, however we can, as long as we're serving life with the gift given to us, within our hearts and our hands, and not serving from our fears. Even if you help just one person, you can't imagine the effect it will have, not only on them, but also the people around them, and future generations.

Outside the restaurant in Bogota that day, I gave Lizzy a hug, and watched them cross the street. When she reached the other side, she paused on the sidewalk holding her son's hand, and waved to me and my family with a glowing smile one last time before they turned the corner. As I watched them walk away, I thought if I could go back in time and if Lizzy were my mother, I would tell her that despite her outward circumstances, she was worthy, and I would thank her for this gift of life she had given me and the opportunity to make my life an inspiration. I would tell her that she should never let fears or circumstances limit the great person she already was, and the even greater person she was becoming. I would tell her that a nice restaurant wasn't just for people who have money, and the things she'd accomplished with her life, you couldn't put a price on them.

The meeting with Lizzy was fuel to my heart, and it began to plant a new seed that would soon reignite the sense of purpose I started out with so many years ago.

Today, I sit here looking out my window as I write the final paragraphs of this book from my home in Waterloo, Ontario. I ended up living in Colombia and Mexico with my wife Johana for over nine years and we loved our life in both countries. During this time, I started a small blog called *Culmen* where I shared my stories and teachings on "Prosperity with Integrity" in Spanish and attracted over half a million readers in a short few years. This gave me the courage to start speaking in Mexico and Colombia as a keynote speaker on the subject of Prosperity with Integrity, teaching professionals the reasons to grow, give, and build their careers and businesses with strong values, ethics and honesty.

It was only five ago from today that my wife, daughter, and I moved from a beautiful small town of Pamplona, Colombia to start our life together here in Canada. After being fired as president of a global company while finishing writing this book, ironically, I find myself standing on the runway of destiny yet again, facing another opportunity, one that has ignited the fire to continue what I started in South America today. Just as in 2006, this next chapter of my life is something that both scares and excites me, all for the greater good.

With this, I don't believe a detour from your path or taking a break is a careless thing. It's an opportunity to evolve for the next chapter. We all need time and patience to reflect and prepare as much as we need gratitude and love to grow and give, all while remembering that God's delays aren't God's denials, and that it's never too late to step out into the rain and feel life shower you with refreshing honesty.

From the whole of my heart and whole of my soul, I encourage you to amplify your own purpose and help someone uncover and amplify theirs, because that's where all of us will find even more joy and love in our lives. Not necessarily for what we specifically want, **but for what all our hearts and spirits thirsts for.**

Thank you for taking this journey with me, and even though we probably haven't met yet, by you picking up this book and reading through to the end, I know you and I are connected either by the lessons we've shared or the stories, experiences, and insights in this words. Either way, I truly wish you the best of life, love and happiness and I look forward to the day our paths will cross and share our perspectives for the greater good - together. God bless.

*"Would now be a good time to take that step you needed
for the greater good?
Or will you continue to make those who need your love,
including yourself, continue to wait?"*
—**Erik Kikuchi**

ABOUT THE AUTHOR

Although as a child, Erik Kikuchi was occasionally homeless and lived in shelters and foster care, he overcame those early challenges and at the age of 24, started his first company which he sold at the age of 31. Thereafter, he went on to build other successful ventures in both Canada and Latin America.

Today, in addition to public speaking and leading his own private consulting practice for CEOs and organizations around the world, Erik Kikuchi is also a passionate home chef who can be found in the kitchen most nights, whipping up four to six course dinners for family and friends.

On a personal note, Kikuchi and his wife Johanna reside in Waterloo, Ontario with their daughter, Elizabeth, and their dog, a Great Pyrenees named Victoria.

Made in the USA
Monee, IL
04 August 2023

40295361R00122